The Universal Gate

Other Works by Venerable Master Hsing Yun:
Life
For All Living Beings
Being Good
Humanistic Buddhism: A Blueprint for Life
Chan Heart, Chan Art
Humble Table, Wise Fare

Sutra Commentaries:
The Rabbit's Horn:
A Commentary on the Platform Sutra
The Great Realizations:
A Commentary on the Eight Realizations
of a Bodhisattva Sutra
Sutra of the Medicine Buddha

The Universal Gate

A Commentary on Avalokitesvara's
Universal Gate Sutra

Venerable Master Hsing Yun

Buddha's Light Publishing, Los Angeles

© 2011 Buddha's Light Publishing
First edition

By Venerable Master Hsing Yun
Cover photograph by David Leung
Book design by Wan Kah Ong and Amanda Ling

Published by Buddha's Light Publishing
3456 S. Glenmark Drive
Hacienda Heights, CA 91745, U.S.A.
Tel: (626) 923-5144
Fax: (626) 923-5145
E-mail: itc@blia.org
Website: www.blpusa.com

Printed in Taiwan.

Library of Congress Cataloging-in-Publication Data

Xingyun, da shi.
  The Universal gate : a commentary on Avalokitesvara's Universal gate sutra / Venerable
Master Hsing Yun.
     p. cm.
  Translated from the Chinese translation of the Sanskrit original.
  "Translated by Robert Smitheram."
  ISBN 978-1-932293-48-7
  1. Tripitaka. Sutrapitaka. Saddharmapundarikasutra. Avalokitesvarasamantamukhap
arivarta—Commentaries. 2. Avalokitesvara (Buddhist deity)—Prayers and devotions.
3. Buddhism—Prayers and devotions. I. Smitheram, Robert. II. Tripitaka. Sutrapitaka.
Saddharmapundarikasutra. Avalokitesvarasamantamukhaparivarta. English. Selections.
III. Title.

  BQ5592.A8X56 2011
  294.3'823--dc22

                              2011006035

Contents

Acknowledgments

Like all of Buddha's Light Publishing's endeavors, this project benefited from the contributions of many people. We would like to thank Venerable Tzu Jung, the Chief Executive of the Fo Guang Shan International Translation Center (FGSITC), Venerble Hui Chi, Abbot of Hsi Lai Temple, and Venerable Yi Chao, Director of FGSITC for their support and leadership.

Robert H. Smitheram provided the translation; John Gill and Louvenia Ortega edited the texts; Susan Tidwell, Tom Manzo, Shujan Cheng proofread the manuscript and prepared it for publication. The book was designed by Wan Kah Ong and Amanda Ling; David Leung provided the cover photograph.

Our appreciation goes to everyone who supported this project from conception to completion.

Editor's Preface

Initially published in Taiwan in 1953, the *Commentary on Avalokitesvara's Universal Gate Sutra* was the first book published by Venerable Master Hsing Yun, and his first success. At age twenty-six, Master Hsing Yun had already contributed to a number of Buddhist periodicals, both as an editor and contributor, including *Raging Billows*, *Splendid Light*, and *Life Monthly*. The success of this commentary cannot be undervalued for building his reputation as a teacher, writer, and Buddhist leader of note in Taiwan.

In the postscript to the first edition, Master Hsing Yun calls his commentary a translation, citing a 1934 commentary written in Japanese by a monastic named Moli Shida, which was provided to him by another monastic named Master Zhidao. Though such a work may have established the interpretive framework for the published commentary, the authorship is substantially Master Hsing Yun's. The commentary features the beginnings of what would come to be known as Master Hsing Yun's style: Buddhist teachings interspersed with humor, history, and poetry, and directly addressing the concerns of the audience.

The present English edition is in many ways more robust than the first edition published over fifty years ago. The text and the sutra have been translated, and the reader has been provided with a glossary of Buddhist terms and a list of the texts cited within the commentary. The Chinese text of the *Universal Gate Sutra* has also been provided as an appendix, accompanied with pinyin pronunciation of each character for chanting.

Etymology is a major concern of the commentary, and perhaps the most difficult to render into English. Instances when words and their meanings are discussed in the abstract have been translated into English, while passages dealing with the concerns of translating Indic and Buddhist concepts into Chinese include some of the Chinese characters in question. This is not meant to be daunting to the English reader, but is provided to make him more aware of the mechanics at play in a text that has been translated through many languages.

The structure of the chapters has been changed in the English edition so that each chapter is of roughly the same size, and some of the larger, quoted sections have been broken up into several smaller ones. This has been done in an attempt to make the text more well-suited for group discussions and Dharma classes. In addition, the margins of the sutra text include the page numbers of the commentary that references that paragraph.

Though published over fifty years ago, Master Hsing Yun's commentary on the *Universal Gate Sutra* has continued to be read and enjoyed in Asia, and it is hoped that this English edition can continue to share this important sutra with a new, ever-widening audience.

Introduction

Though he is called *Guanyin* in China, *Kannon* in Japan, and *Gwan-eum* in Korea, regardless of the name, there is no one in these countries who is not familiar with Avalokitesvara Bodhisattva. In these countries the belief in Avalokitesvara is not found only in Buddhist monasteries and nunneries, nor is it limited exclusively to Buddhists. Wherever people live, be it in cities or rural villages, upon remote mountain tops or along the seashore, just about every family keeps and venerates a statue of Avalokitesvara Bodhisattva.

How has Avalokitesvara Bodhisattva become the focus of faith for so many people? The Buddhist teachings make mention of numerous bodhisattvas; the *Lotus Sutra* itself mentions an assembly that contains more than eighty thousand bodhisattvas. Among this assembly eighteen great bodhisattvas are specifically named, and even among these eighteen there are some bodhisattvas whom no one especially venerates and of which very little is known. Yet among these, Avalokitesvara Bodhisattva has become the bodhisattva that everyone knows about and believes in.

1

Why? Such answers can be found by reading the *Universal Gate Sutra*.

The *Lotus Sutra*, whose full title is the *Lotus Flower of the Wondrous Dharma Sutra*, is a magnificent sutra which describes Sakyamuni Buddha's reason for appearing in the world. The *Universal Gate Sutra* just mentioned is only one of the twenty-eight chapters of the *Lotus Sutra*. The *Universal Gate Sutra* provides a description of Avalokitesvara Bodhisattva and how he serves as a "universal gate" of benefits for sentient beings. Because of its specificity and popularity, the *Universal Gate Sutra* is often chanted on its own, and circulates as a separate text.

Originally written in Sanskrit, the translation of the *Lotus Sutra* discussed within was translated into Chinese by Kumarajiva (344-413), a Buddhist monk who lived during the Later Qin dynasty. Kumarajiva is considered one of the four great Buddhist translators of China, the other three being Paramartha (499-569), Xuanzang (602-664), and Amoghavajra (705-774). Among these four, Kumarajiva occupies an extremely important position both in terms of his understanding of the teachings and his skill as a translator. In the case of the *Lotus Sutra*, several other translations appeared both before and after Kumarajiva's, but Kumarajiva's version has remained the most popular and widely circulated. Additionally, when Master Zhizhe (538-597) founded the Tiantai School, a Buddhist school whose central text is the *Lotus Sutra*, he did so based upon Kumarajiva's translation. Such details only further illuminate the extraordinary qualities of Kumarajiva and the innovations of his translation.

Kumarajiva was born in Qiuci, a central Asian country that is now part of China's Western Regions. At the age of seven he went with his mother to visit many famous Buddhist teachers and thoroughly studied the Buddhist sutras. Of special interest to Kumarajiva were the teachings of Nagarjuna (150-250), whose perspective on *prajna* wisdom can be seen in Kumarajiva's translation of the *Lotus Sutra*. Among Kumarajiva's disciples were Sengrui (ca. 4th-5th cent.) and Daosheng (355-434), both of whose teachings led to the establishment of the Tiantai School.

When Kumarajiva first arrived in China more than fifteen hundred years ago, China was experiencing chaos wrought by the nomadic tribes to the north, forcing the Jin court south. At this time the capital of Jianye (modern Nanjing) was established on the lower reaches of the Yangzi River—later called the Eastern Jin dynasty. At the time, the commanding general, Fu Jian (337-385), declared himself emperor of an independent state in Changan (modern Xian) within the Yellow River Valley, which he called Qin and which later historians would call the Former Qin dynasty. His general, Lü Guang (337-399), employed his military prowess to subdue various parts of the Western Regions, and received orders to welcome Kumarajiva to China, but soon after, Fu Jian was hit by a stray arrow during the Battle of Fei River, and later died. With the end of his rule, Yao Chang (331-394) assumed power. This period would later be known as the Later Qin, or Yao-Qin.

Lü Guang learned of the death of Fu Jian while on the road during a distant campaign, and as he had been consistently victorious throughout the Western Regions, he established his own state in present-day Gansu Province, known as the Later Liang dynasty. At the time, Kumarajiva had arrived at Guzang, the capital of the Later Liang dynasty. Later on, the Yao-Qin dynasty's second ruler, Yao Xing (366-416), ascended the throne and became a devout follower of Buddhism. Yao Xing lavished Kumarajiva with gifts and, in the third year of the Hongshi era (401), welcomed him to

Changan, constructing Ximing Hall for Kumarajiva to live in and Xiaoyao Garden to serve as his translation center. This inaugurated a glorious period in Chinese Buddhist history.

The combination of Kumarajiva's scholarship and moral prestige and Yao Xing's patronage allowed the translation center at Xiaoyao Garden to be truly astonishing. The translation center was staffed with over three thousand individuals: about two thousand individuals participated in the translation of the *Lotus Sutra*, about two thousand individuals participated in the translation of the *Sutra Asked by Visesacinta Brahma Deva*, and about thirteen hundred individuals participated in the translation of the *Vimalakirti Sutra*. Other Buddhist scriptures like the *Perfection of Great Wisdom Sutra*, the *Diamond Sutra*, and the *Amitabha Sutra* were all translated under such splendid conditions.

The *Lotus Sutra* was translated in 406, six years after Kumarajiva's arrival in Changan. Kumarajiva's translation originally consisted of only twenty-seven chapters, with the Devadatta Chapter added some eighty years later and jointly translated by Dharmamati (ca. late 5th cent.) and Faxian (423-497). At that time Kumarajiva's translation contained prose only, and did not yet feature the repetitions in verse. It was not until some one hundred and eighty years later that the verses were added by Jnanagupta (523-600) that the *Lotus Sutra* became the version that circulates today.

Commentaries on the *Lotus Sutra* were authored in India very early on, with Vasubandhu's commentary appearing in the fourth century. There was a also a profusion of Chinese *Lotus Sutra* commentaries, written by adherents of several Buddhist schools, including Fayun of the Nirvana School's *Annotations on the Meaning of the Lotus Sutra*, Jiaxiang Jizang of the Three Treatise Schools' *Annotations on the Meaning of the Lotus Sutra*, Cien Kuiji of the Faxiang School's *Analysis and Appreciation of the Lotus Sutra,* and Jiehuan of the Chan School's *Explanation of the Lotus Sutra.* Zhizhe also wrote three major works on the *Lotus Sutra*: the *Profound Meaning of the Lotus Sutra,* the *Exegesis on the Words and Phrases in the Lotus Sutra,* and the *Great Stopping and Seeing.* One can see that the *Lotus Sutra* occupies a very important position across many schools of Buddhism, such that its value cannot be ignored.

Mahayana and Hinayana

The development of Buddhism can be divided into two periods: "Early Buddhism" and "Later Buddhism." There were many early Buddhist schools, but they can all be categorized as Hinayana, or "small vehicle" schools. Early Buddhism saw the phenomena of the universe as empty, impermanent, and filled with suffering, and thus as something to be escaped from. Early Buddhism's goal was to renounce the world and strive to liberate oneself from it. Benefiting and helping others was not a concern. Such people are called "selfish practitioners." Their goal is self-liberation, for they do not perceive a relationship between the liberation of others and themselves.

Later Buddhism, also called Mahayana, or "Great Vehicle," marked a reversal of this kind of thinking. Mahayana Buddhism sees the phenomena of the universe as reality itself, asserting that our actions and our principles can be perfectly intertwined, and that self and other are equal. Where Hinayana is passive, Mahayana is active. Where Hinayana is staid, Mahayana is dynamic. Where Hinayana is individualistic, Mahayana is social.

Within Mahayana Buddhism there is also a distinction between skillful means and absolute teachings. In this context, "skillful means" refers to provisional teachings given to suit the limited capacity of those learning them. Such teachings do not provide a complete exposition of non-duality, and as such, describe different levels and varieties of enlightenment. Absolute teachings do not speak of such differences, for as the *Lotus Sutra* says, "There is only one Dharma, not two, and not three." All the phenomena in the universe are manifestations of the wondrous Dharma of the Middle Way in its true form.

The ancient Buddhist sages understood that one is all, and would say, "The green willow is the Buddha's pure and wondrous Dharma body, while the wind blowing through the pine and cypress is the sound of all the Buddhas and bodhisattvas teaching the Dharma, liberating living beings."

Flowing water speaks the words of the Buddha; the mountain scene is none other than his pure body. Such descriptions capture the non-duality of the absolute teachings. Among all sutras, the *Lotus Sutra* describes this principle best, which is why it is regarded as the greatest of all Mahayana sutras.

According to Buddhist tradition, when Sakyamuni Buddha first began to teach in the world, he intended to start the "wheel of the essential Dharma turning" by delivering the teachings contained within the *Flower Adornment Sutra*. But such profound ideas are not easily absorbed by most common people, and thus the Buddha applied skillful means and began with the more basic teachings from the *Agama Sutras*, then later the more advanced and Mahayana-like *Vaipulya Sutras*, and finally onto the *prajna* teachings. In this manner the Buddha used skillful means to lead people, step by step, to the absolute Mahayana teachings. Ultimately, at a gathering that would come to be known as the "lotus assembly," the Buddha did away with skillful means and delivered the absolute teachings in the *Lotus Sutra*. Only at this point could Sakyamuni Buddha's goal of teaching the path to enlightenment be considered to have been truly accomplished.

The teachings of the *Lotus Sutra* were delivered by Sakyamuni Buddha late in his life at a place called Vulture Peak northeast of the city of Rajagrha. At that time a massive assembly had gathered at Vulture Peak, including eighty thousand great bodhisattvas headed by Manjusri and Avalokitesvara, and twelve thousand great arhats headed by Mahakasyapa and Sariputra, among others. The eight classes of celestial beings were also present: *devas, nagas, yaksas, gandharvas, asuras, garudas, kimnaras,* and *mahoragas.* Also in attendance were Buddhist followers among the royal families, such as kings, ministers, wealthy patrons, and scholars. All of these beings gathered at the assembly on Vulture Peak to listen to Sakyamuni Buddha preach the Dharma.

Not including the teachings of the *Flower Adornment Sutra*, those teachings delivered in the middle period leading up to the *Lotus Sutra* can be grouped together as provisional teachings. Only the teachings delivered at the lotus assembly represent the essence of the Dharma, and are called "the Dharma wheel that forgoes the provisional and returns to the essence." This shows the important place that the *Lotus Sutra* occupies within the entirety of the Buddhist sutras.

The *Lotus Sutra* is divided into twenty-eight chapters. Each chapter is important, and none should be considered greater or lesser than the others, but for the sake of convenience the various chapters can be analyzed and grouped. One way to do so is to divide the sutra into two parts: manifestations and essentials. The first fourteen chapters of the *Lotus Sutra* comprise the part on manifestations, and are concerned with Sakyamuni Buddha's physical manifestations in the world. The final fourteen chapters of the *Lotus Sutra* comprise the part on essentials, as they elucidate the essentials of Sakyamuni Buddha's teachings and describe the message he wished to give to the world: that he was a manifestation of the truth of the universe, and that he had attained Buddhahood long ago.

There are four chapters in the *Lotus Sutra* which are most commonly read and studied: The Skillful Means Chapter and the Peaceful Practicing Chapter, which belong to the part on manifestations, and the Lifespan of the Tathagata Chapter and the Universal Gate Chapter, which belong to the part on essentials. Miaoyue Zhanran (711-782), the ninth patriarch of the Tiantai School, said of these four chapters:

> The Skillful Means Chapter is the aspiration for enlightenment, the Peaceful Practicing Chapter is cultivation, the Lifespan of the Tathagata Chapter is *bodhi*, and the Universal Gate Chapter is *nirvana*.

From Miaoyue Zhanran's analysis we can see just how important the Universal Gate Chapter is within the *Lotus Sutra*. The fact that the recitation of Avalokitesvara's name has become a focus of practice and that the image of Avalokitesvara has become an object of veneration for people everywhere begins to make perfect sense.

Lotus Flower of the Wondrous Dharma Sutra

The title of a Buddhist sutra provides a general outline of the text and encompasses the main ideas that are covered within it. In particular, it could be said that the five characters that constitute the full Chinese title of the *Lotus Sutra* embody the truth of the entire universe and encapsulate the meaning of the Buddha's eighty-four thousand teachings, including the essence of the entire Buddhist canon of some fifty-five hundred sutras. A detailed explanation of these five characters could even encompass the three great treatises of the Tiantai School.

妙	法	蓮	華	經
miao	*fa*	*lian*	*hua*	*jing*
Wondrous	Dharma	Lotus	Flower	Scripture
Saddharma		*Pundarika*		*Sutra*

Wondrous Dharma

The first two characters of the *Lotus Sutra* are *miao fa*, meaning "wondrous Dharma." The specific wondrous teachings mentioned in the title are the "ten realms and the ten qualities." The ten realms are a grouping of ten different means of possible rebirth, and include hell, the realm of hungry ghosts, the animal realm, the *asura* realm, the human realm, heaven, the realm of *sravakas*, the realm of *pratyekabuddhas*, the realm of bodhisattvas, and the realm of Buddhas.

The Ten Qualities

1. Form
2. Nature
3. Entity
4. Ability
5. Activity
6. Causes
7. Conditions
8. Direct Effects
9. Indirect Effects
10. Complete from Beginning to End

In each of the realms are found ten qualities. In Chinese, these ten qualities are called *shi rushi* (十如是) "ten such as they are," for each quality is causally related to and influences the other qualities. For example, if the quality of form is wholesome, the quality of effect will be such as well, and if the quality of form is unwholesome, the effect will be unwholesome as well. To understand these ten qualities, consider the human realm: human beings each have an external, physical form, this is the quality of "form." However, each human form possesses its characteristics and inherent nature, this is the quality of "nature." When form and nature are present together, this is the third quality, "entity." Any given entity will have certain things it can do, and this is the quality of "ability." These abilities allow us to act upon the external world, and these actions are the quality of "activity." Our activities, or behavior, then create our karmic causes, which is the quality of "causes," and alongside this quality exists the quality of "conditions," which help to fulfill or allow these causes to result in the quality of "direct effects." One example of a direct effect is a human birth, for each person has been born as a human because of the causes in previous lifetimes. Yet there are still karmic differences among people: some are rich, some are poor, some are wise, some are foolish, some are happy, and some are unhappy. These differences are the quality of "indirect effects." Each of these qualities, from "form" in the beginning to "indirect effects" in the end is an eternal truth governed by natural laws. They will not change no matter what happens, and thus exhibit the quality of "complete from beginning to end." These ten qualities that are present in the human realm are found in the other nine realms as well.

The Causes of the Ten Realms

The Hell Realm:	Anger
The Realm of Hungry Ghosts:	Greed
The Animal Realm:	Ignorance
The *Asura* Realm:	Jealousy
The Human Realm:	The Five Precepts
The Heavenly Realm:	Ten Wholesome Actions
The *Sravaka* Realm:	Four Noble Truths
The *Pratyekabuddha* Realm:	Dependent Origination
The Bodhisattva Realm:	Six Perfections
The Buddha Realm:	Complete Enlightenment

Furthermore, each of the ten realms individually contains within it all ten realms. This is possible because all ten realms are governed by the nature of inclusiveness and the nature of causality. Allow me to explain:

If we were to take a critical look into our own hearts, we would see that we generate the causes for each of the ten realms within a single day. But are most of these the wholesome thoughts of the Buddhas and bodhisattvas, or the unwholesome thoughts of hell-beings and hungry ghosts? When we get out of bed each morning, our minds feel like the rising sun, imbued with the freshness of the morning sky. But by breakfast, we may already be having thoughts of dissatisfaction, depending on how good or bad our meal is. With a thought of anger, we create hell in our minds. When we quarrel with our neighbors or family members, we create the realm of *asuras,* who fight among themselves. When we feel the pangs of hunger, we create the realm of hungry ghosts. People are easily controlled by the external environment in this way.

There is a Confucian maxim that says, "Reflect upon yourself thrice daily." This potential for reflection and improvement is evidence that we all have "Buddha nature," the inherent quality to become Buddhas. The Buddha realm's wisdom begins right here in the human realm in our Buddha nature. In the same way, we can compare the other nine realms to ourselves and clearly see how the human realm contains the ten realms. By extension we can surmise that each of the other nine realms contains the ten realms; this is called the "nature of inclusiveness."

The ten realms are, by nature, inclusive, which means that each realm contains all ten realms within it. However, each of the ten realms is subject to the nature of causality. For example, hell contains the other nine realms within it because of its inclusive nature, including the wholesome realms of humans, *sravakas, pratyeka-buddhas*, bodhisattvas, and Buddhas, but despite this inclusion, the beings in hell have unwholesome thoughts, and taking such thoughts as karmic causes they are reborn in hell.

In the same way, the Buddha realm contains the other nine realms in the sense of the nature of inclusion, though according to the nature of causality it is distinct. One is able to become a Buddha because one only gives rise to wholesome thoughts, and this leads to Buddhahood. This way of understanding the ten realms is one of the wondrous teachings of the Tiantai School, and we should continually bear it in mind. This is not simply a theory, but can be of practical application to our spiritual practice.

In this sense, to call these teachings "wondrous" is to say that they cannot be fully conceptualized. Whether called the "ten realms" or the "ten qualities," all such teachings describe those natural laws which govern each and every thought. It is important to note that here the term "natural law" refers to cause and effect, not the theories discussed outside of the Buddhist context. The ten qualities mentioned earlier are just a particular enumeration of the law of cause and effect. When we see how the ten realms are manifested in our own lives, can we call this teaching anything other than wondrous?

These laws were not created by the Buddha, but are simply natural laws. If you generate the causes for rebirth into hell, then you will experience the karmic effect of becoming a hell being, whether you like it or not. If you generate the causes leading to the animal realm, then you will become an animal. In the same way, good causes lead to good results with the same level of certainty. These natural laws exist throughout the past, present, and future. There is truly no way to describe this other than "wondrous."

It is important that we do not view the wondrous Dharma simply as a set of philosophical principles. It is best to view teachings like the ten realms and the ten qualities as particular enumerations of the truth, delivered to aid us in practice. If we maintain this perspective, we can treat them as truth.

If we look at our minds in light of the wondrous Dharma as described above, then we can see that the causes that elevate or lower us through the ten realms originate completely within the ignorance or enlightenment of the mind, for nothing is beyond the law of cause and effect. If we can see the world clearly in this way, then we can discover the incredible significance of Avalokitesvara Bodhisattva's many manifestations to benefit and help beings as described in the *Universal Gate Sutra* and gain a greater understanding of the practice of reciting this bodhisattva's name with great devotion.

Lotus Flower

The next two characters in the Chinese title of the Sutra are *lianhua*, or "lotus flower." What is the significance of the name "lotus flower" in the title of the sutra? The Sanskrit title of the sutra is *Saddharma Pundarika Sutra.* Though the second Sanskrit compound is translated as "lotus flower," the more precise translation would be "white lotus."

The lotus flower functions as a Buddhist symbol in two ways. First, a lotus flower grows in the mud, but blossoms above the water, unsullied. In the same way, though rooted in the world, the Dharma is pure. Second, a lotus possesses both a blossom and its fruit at the same time. While most plants blossom first and then bear fruit when the blossom has fallen away, the lotus has a platform for its fruit within its calyx as it blossoms. In the same way, according to the wondrous Dharma, cause and effect are not separate: there are causes within effects and effects within causes. For example, the ignorance of beings within the nine lower realms can be seen as a cause, and the enlightenment of the Buddha realm is its effect. However, since each realm contains all ten realms, the realms of living beings contain the Buddha realm just as the Buddha realm contains the realms of living beings. Thus there is no duality between living beings and Buddhas.

---

*For a full explication of the Sanskrit title of the sutra, see chapter eight of *Zhizhe's Analytical Commentary on the Lotus Sutra.*

Sutra

"Sutra" is a Sanskrit term that is best translated as "concordant scripture," in the sense that it describes a scripture which accords with the Buddha's teachings and also accords with the capacity of living beings. The word "sutra" also has two other meanings: "to connect together" and "to support completely." The first meaning, "to connect together," is relevant because all sutras are fundamentally consistent in meaning, while the second meaning, "to embrace completely," refers to how the Buddha embraces and liberates all living beings universally, omitting none. The Chinese translation of *sutra* is *jing* (經), "classic," which was selected to emphasize that the Buddha's teachings do not change over time.

The reasoning behind the title of the sutra, "Lotus Flower of the Wondrous Dharma," is well described in the Skillful Means Chapter of the *Lotus Sutra*. Of the sutra it says:

> Such a teaching is taught by the Tathagatas at certain [rare] times, just as the *udumbara* flower appears on [rare] occasions.

The "udumbara flower" is the Sanskrit name of a legendarily auspicious flower that can be translated as "blue lotus flower." The flower does not normally appear in the world, but it is said that when a Buddha or a wheel-turning monarch appears in the world, the udumbara flower appears. In the same way, the Buddha's revelation of the teachings of the *Lotus Sutra* is like the blossoming of a rare and auspicious flower.

Avalokitesvara Bodhisattva

The name "Avalokitesvara" is made up of three major components in Sanskrit:

- *ārya*: An honorific, commonly translated as "noble."
- *avalokita*: To contemplate or observe.
- *īśvara*: Meaning "mastery" or "flexibility" when taken as an adjective, "lord" or "master" when taken as a noun.

The name of Avalokitesvara Bodhisattva has been translated from the Sanskirt in various ways. Kumarajiva translated it as *guanshiyin* (觀世音), meaning "observing the sounds of the world." Predating Kumarajiva, Dharmaraksa translated it as *guangshiyin* (光世音), meaning "bringing light to the sounds of the world." By Xuanzang's time it was translated as *guanzizai* (觀自在), meaning "observing at ease." Which translation is correct?

Xuangzang's translation corresponds very closely to the Sanskrit. His translation of "observing at ease" corresponds to both the nounal and verbal meaning of *isvara*, and is thus more correct. That is why Xuanzang states in his biography that the old translations of *guangshiyin* and *guanshiyin* are both incorrect.

However, does this really mean that Kumarajiva's translation is a mistake? Kumarajiva's style of translation is to paraphrase the meaning of a sutra rather than offer a literal translation. If we look at the vow of Avalokitesvara Bodhisattva as described by Sakyamuni Buddha in the sutra, we can see that Kumarajiva is not mistaken:

The Buddha answered Aksayamati Bodhisattva, "Good men, if there be countless hundreds of millions of billions of living beings experiencing all manner of suffering who hear of Avalokitesvara Bodhisattva and call his name with single-minded effort, then Avalokitesvara Bodhisattva will instantly observe the sound of their cries, and they will all be liberated."

Kumarajiva's translation of *guanshiyin,* "observing the sounds of the world" is thus taken from this passage. We can then see the importance of this section of the sutra.

According to the Esoteric School, Avalokitesvara embodies the Buddha's virtue of great compassion, and is depicted as the main disciple of Amitabha Buddha while he was still practicing as a bodhisattva. Amitabha Buddha is usually described as having two main attendants: Avalokitesvara and Mahasthamaprapta. Avalokitesvara Bodhisattva presides over the teaching of compassion, while Mahasthamaprapta Bodhisattva presides over that of wisdom.

Xuanzang's translation, "observing at ease," was selected to reflect how this bodhisattva wishes to ensure that living beings can attain ease by observing all phenomena. Kumarajiva's translation, "observing the sounds of the world," was selected because Avalokitesvara Bodhisattva observes and hears those living beings who single-mindedly call his name and comes to liberate them from the misery of the world. Thus, both the translations of Kumarajiva and Xuanzang are apt and meaningful.

The Pure Land

A "Pure Land" is a realm created through the power of a bodhisattva's vows where the Dharma can be practiced without worldly obstructions. There are many pure lands, and Avalokitesvara is described as presiding over a Pure Land called Potalaka. According to the last chapter of *Huiyuan's Dictionary*:

> "Mount Potalaka" means "mountain with a forest of little flowers." On this mountain there are many trees with little white flowers. The flowers are very fragrant, and their perfume carries a great distance.

The nineteenth chapter of the *Inquiry into the Profundity of the Flower Adornment Sutra* states:

> The place named Mount Potalaka in India lacks an accepted translation, but a translation of its meaning would be "mountain adorned with little trees and vines."

The name of this mountain is also mentioned in the *Eleven Faces Sutra* and the *Flower Adornment Sutra*.

Since belief in Avalokitesvara Bodhisattva is so prominent in East Asia, many places named after Potalaka can be found throughout the region. The Zhoushan archipelago in southern China is home to Mount Putuo, one of the Four Great Mountains of Chinese Buddhism, and is called the seat of enlightenment of Avalokitesvara Bodhisattva. Potala Palace, the Dalai Lama's temporal seat in Tibet's capital of Lhasa, is also derived from Potalaka, as the Dalai Lama is said to be a manifestation of Avalokitesvara. The *Universal Gate Sutra* describes part of Avalokitesvara's vow to completely transform this world into Potalaka.

Avalokitesvara Bodhisattva has many other names and titles throughout the Buddhist sutras. Other names found within the *Universal Gate Sutra* include "Bestower of Fearlessness" and "Pure and Noble One." The *Sutra on Invoking Avalokitesvara Bodhisattva* calls Avalokitesvara the "Compassionate Bestower of Fearlessness." The *Flower of Compassion Sutra* calls Avalokitesvara the "Tathagata who Clearly Understands the True Dharma" and the "Tathagata who Subsumes the Highest Peak of all Merit and Virtue." The *Sutra on the Prophesized Enlightenment of Avalokitesvara Bodhisattva* calls Avalokitesvara the "Compassionate Noble One," the "Liberator of those in Misery," and "Buddha of Universal Light and the Highest Peak of Merit and Virtue." The *Mantra Ritual* calls Avalokitesvara the "Lord of Great Compassion," and the *Vajra Realm Mandala* names him the "Vajra Bodhisattva."

Bodhisattva

"Bodhisattva" is a Sanskrit word that is transliterated into Chinese as *putisaduo*, though more commonly shortened to just *pusa* (菩薩). When first translated into Chinese, "bodhisattva" was rendered as *dadao xin zhongsheng*, "living being with a great aspiration for enlightenment." Later translations rendered the word as *jue youqing*, "awakened being." The first chapter of Sengzhao's (384-414) *Annotations to the Vimalakirti Sutra* describes the etymology as follows:

> *Pusa* is the Chinese abbreviation for the name *bodhisattva*. "Bodhi" means "the path to Buddhahood,"

and *sattva* can be translated as "living being with a great aspiration," for only those with great aspiration can enter the path to Buddhahood. Thus they are called "bodhisattva."

The Abhidharma canon states:

> *Bodhi* means supreme enlightenment and *sattva* means great aspiration. The word refers to someone who generates the great, vast aspiration to seek supreme enlightenment and liberate living beings. Thus they are called "bodhisattva."

The *Treatise on the Perfection of Great Wisdom* states:

> *Bodhi* means "the Buddha Way," and *sattva* means "bringing liberation to living beings," so that one liberates living beings by applying the Buddha Way. Thus they are called "bodhisattva."

It also states:

> *Bodhi* is self-cultivation and *sattva* is transforming others. One who engages in the self-cultivation of Buddhahood in order to liberate living beings is called a bodhisattva.

However, the explication found in the Abhidharma differs somewhat from that found in the *Treatise on the Perfection of Great Wisdom*. In the passage from the Abhidharma, a bodhisattva is interpreted as one who vows to seek supreme enlightenment for the sake of all living beings. This is similar to the general understanding of a bodhisattva as a being who seeks enlightenment from the Buddhas in order to liberate beings. In this interpretation, a bodhisattva has not yet attained enlightenment. However, the language of the *Treatise on the Perfection of Great Wisdom* states that bodhisattvas "apply the Buddha Way," implying that they have already attained enlightenment. In this explanation bodhisattvas have already attained enlightenment, and having attained enlightenment, are able to provide the best medicine for the illnesses of living beings.

The *Great Compassion Dharani* describes Avalokitesvara Bodhisattva as having attained Buddhahood long ago as a Buddha named "Tathagata who Clearly Understands the True Dharma." It is because of his great compassion that he manifests once again as a bodhisattva to liberate beings as the proper conditions arise. This is very different from the average being who seeks a higher level of enlightenment. Thus, when comparing these two explications of the word *bodhisattva*, the *Treatise on the Perfection of Great Wisdom* is more accurate.

Universal Gate

The word "universal" in the title Universal Gate refers to how Avalokitesvara Bodhisattva embodies all virtues universally. Actually, Avalokitesvara not only embodies all virtues universally but also dynamically applies the powers of compassion and liberation. Thus "universal" means that he is able to universally manifest the light of compassionate liberation everywhere.

The Chinese character for "gate," *men* (門), carries the additional meanings of "group" or "classification," and thus refers to the many groups of beings that are liberated by Avalokitesvara Bodhisattva. Thus "universal gate" refers to Avalokitesvara's ability to universally respond to living beings without exception, even though they vary in many ways. Such expanse invokes a certain ancient Chinese couplet:

> The moon shines over a thousand running rivers,
> The sky extends for endless miles.

Perhaps this is the best way to depict Avalokitesvara Bodhisattva's method for evoking his universal gate of thirty-three manifestations.

Avalokitesvara's Universal Gate Sutra

At that time, Aksayamati Bodhisattva rose from his seat, bared 38
his right shoulder, put his palms together facing the Buddha, and
said, "World-honored One, for what reason is Avalokitesvara 39
Bodhisattva named 'Observing the Sounds of the World'?"

The Buddha answered Aksayamati Bodhisattva, "Good men, if 40
there be countless hundreds of millions of billions of living beings
experiencing all manner of suffering who hear of Avalokitesvara
Bodhisattva and call his name with single-minded effort, then
Avalokitesvara Bodhisattva will instantly observe the sound of
their cries, and they will all be liberated.

"If anyone who upholds the name of Avalokitesvara Bodhi- 51
sattva were to fall into a great fire, the fire would be unable to burn
that person due to the bodhisattva's awe-inspiring spiritual powers.
If anyone, carried away by a flood, were to call his name, that per- 55
son would immediately reach a shallow place.

"If there are living beings in the hundreds of millions of billions 58
who go out to sea in search of such treasures as gold, silver, lapis
lazuli, mother of pearl, carnelian, coral, amber, and pearls, and if a

23

fierce storm were to blow their ship off course to make landfall in the territory of *raksas,* and further if among them there is even one person who calls the name of Avalokitesvara Bodhisattva, then all of those people will be liberated from the torment of the *raksas.* This is why the bodhisattva is named "Observing the Sounds of the World."

62   "Or if someone facing imminent attack calls the name of Avalokitesvara Bodhisattva, the knives and clubs held by the attackers will then break into pieces, and that person will attain liberation.

65   "If a great three thousand-fold world system was full of *yaksas* and *raksas* seeking to torment people, and they heard someone call the name of Avalokitesvara Bodhisattva, these evil demons would not even be able to see that person with their evil eyes, much less do any harm.

68   "Or if someone, whether guilty or not guilty, who is bound and fettered with manacles, shackles, and cangue calls the name of Avalokitesvara Bodhisattva, then all the bonds will be broken, and that person will instantly attain liberation.

71   "If a great three thousand-fold world system were full of malevolent brigands, and a merchant chief were leading many merchants carrying valuable treasures along a perilous road, and among them one man were to speak up and said, "Good men, do not be afraid. You should call the name of Avalokitesvara Bodhisattva with single-minded effort, for this bodhisattva can bestow fearlessness upon living beings. If you call his name, then you will surely be liberated from these malevolent brigands!" and upon hearing this, if all of the merchants were to call out: "I take refuge in Avalokitesvara Bodhisattva," then by calling his name, they would instantly attain liberation.

75   "Aksayamati, lofty indeed are the awe-inspiring spiritual powers of the great Avalokitesvara Bodhisattva.

"If any living beings are much given to greed, let them keep   77
in mind and revere Avalokitesvara Bodhisattva, and they will be
freed from their greed.

"If any are much given to anger, let them keep in mind and re-   80
vere Avalokitesvara Bodhisattva, and they will be freed from their
anger.

"If any are much given to ignorance, let them keep in mind and   83
revere Avalokitesvara Bodhisattva, and they will be freed from
their ignorance.

"Aksayamati, Avalokitesvara Bodhisattva possesses such awe-   85
inspiring spiritual powers, and many have benefited from them.
This is why living beings should constantly keep him in mind.

"If any woman wishes for a male child by worshipping and   87
making offerings to Avalokitesvara Bodhisattva, she will then
give birth to a son blessed with merit and wisdom. If she wishes
for a female child, she will then give birth to a daughter blessed
with well-formed and attractive features, one who has planted the
roots of virtue over lifetimes and is cherished and respected by all.
Aksayamati, such are the powers of Avalokitesvara Bodhisattva!

"If any living being reveres and worships Avalokitesvara   91
Bodhisattva, their auspicious merit will not have been in vain.

"Therefore, let all living beings accept and uphold the name   93
of Avalokitesvara Bodhisattva. Aksayamati, suppose someone
were to accept and uphold the names of as many bodhisattvas as
there are grains of sand along sixty-two hundred million Ganges
rivers, and spend a lifetime in making offerings of food, drink,
clothing, lodging, and medicines to them. What do you think?
Would the merit for such a good man or good woman be great or
not?"

Aksayamati replied, "Great indeed, World-honored One."

94   The Buddha said, "Suppose there is another person who accepts and upholds the name of Avalokitesvara Bodhisattva, and worships and makes offerings to him for a single moment; the merit gained by these two people will be exactly the same without any difference. Such merit cannot be exhausted even in hundreds of millions of billions of kalpas. Aksayamati, such are the immeasurable and limitless benefits of the auspicious merit one obtains from accepting and upholding the name of Avalokitesvara Bodhisattva."

99   Aksayamati Bodhisattva said to the Buddha, "World-honored One, how did Avalokitesvara Bodhisattva come to this Saha World? How does he teach the Dharma for the sake of living beings? How does he apply the power of skillful means?"

101   The Buddha told Aksayamati Bodhisattva, "Good men, if there are living beings in this land who should be liberated by someone in the form of a Buddha, then Avalokitesvara Bodhisattva will manifest in the form of a Buddha and teach the Dharma to them."

102   "For those who should be liberated by someone in the form of a *pratyekabuddha*, then he will manifest in the form of a *pratyekabuddha* and teach the Dharma to them. For those who should be liberated by someone in the form of a *sravaka*, then he will manifest in the form of a *sravaka* and teach the Dharma to them.

106   "For those who should be liberated by someone in the form of King Brahma, then he will manifest in the form of King Brahma and teach the Dharma to them. For those who should be liberated by someone in the form of Lord Sakra, then he will manifest in the form of Lord Sakra and teach the Dharma to them. For those who should be liberated by someone in the form of Isvara, then he will manifest in the form of Isvara and teach the Dharma to them.

111   "For those who should be liberated by someone in the form of the Mahesvara, then he will manifest in the form of the Mahesvara

and teach the Dharma to them. For those who should be liberated by someone in the form of a great heavenly general, then he will manifest in the form of a great heavenly general and teach the Dharma to them. For those who should be liberated by someone in the form of Vaisravana, then he will manifest in the form of Vaisravana and teach the Dharma to them.

"For those who should be liberated by someone in the form of   114
a lesser king, then he will manifest in the form of a lesser king and teach the Dharma to them. For those who should be liberated by someone in the form of an elder, then he will manifest in the form of an elder and teach the Dharma to them. For those who should be liberated by someone in the form of a layperson, then he will manifest in the form of a layperson and teach the Dharma to them. For those who should be liberated by someone in the form of a minister, then he will manifest in the form of a minister and teach the Dharma to them. For those who should be liberated by someone in the form of a brahman, then he will manifest in the form of a brahman and teach the Dharma to them.

"For those who should be liberated by someone in the form of   119
a *bhiksu*, a *bhiksuni*, an *upasaka*, or an *upasika*, then he will manifest in the form of a *bhiksu*, a *bhiksuni*, an *upasaka*, or an *upasika* and teach the Dharma to them.

"For those who should be liberated by someone in the form   122
of a woman who is an elder, a layperson, a minister, or a brahman, then he will manifest in the form of a woman and teach the Dharma to them.

"For those who should be liberated by someone in the form of   123
a young boy or young girl, then he will manifest in the form of a young boy or young girl and teach the Dharma to them.

129   "For those who should be liberated by someone in such forms as a *deva*, a *naga*, a *yaksa*, a *gandharva*, an *asura*, a *garuda*, a *kimnara*, a *mahoraga*, human or nonhuman being, then he will manifest in all these forms and teach the Dharma to them.

132   "For those who should be liberated by a vajrapani deity, then he will manifest as a vajrapani deity and teach the Dharma to them.

134   "Aksayamati, such is the merit that Avalokitesvara Bodhisattva has accomplished, and the various forms in which he wanders the various lands bringing liberation to living beings.

135   "This is why all of you should single-mindedly make offerings to Avalokitesvara Bodhisattva, for it is the great Avalokitesvara Bodhisattva who can bestow fearlessness in the midst of terror and in dire circumstances. This is why everyone in this Saha World calls him the bestower of fearlessness."

138   Aksayamati Bodhisattva said to the Buddha, "World-honored One, now I must make an offering to Avalokitesvara Bodhisattva." Then he took from his neck a necklace of numerous precious gems worth thousands of ounces in gold, and gave it to him saying, "Kind one, accept this necklace of precious gems as a Dharma gift."

140   At the time, Avalokitesvara Bodhisattva was unwilling to accept it. Aksayamati spoke once more to Avalokitesvara Bodhisattva, "Kind one, accept this necklace as a kindness to us."

141   Then the Buddha said to Avalokitesvara Bodhisattva, "Accept this jeweled necklace out of compassion for Aksayamati Bodhisattva, as well as the four groups of Buddhist disciples, the *devas, nagas, yaksas, gandharvas, asuras, garudas, kimnaras, mahoragas*, human or nonhuman beings." Thereupon, Avalokitesvara Bodhisattva accepted the jeweled necklace out of compassion for the four groups of Buddhist disciples, the *devas* and *nagas*, and

the human and nonhuman beings, and dividing it into two parts, presented one part to Sakyamuni Buddha and presented the other part to the stupa of Prabhutaratna Buddha.

"Aksayamati, it is with such freely exercised spiritual pow-   144
ers that Avalokitesvara Bodhisattva wanders through the Saha World."

Then Aksayamati Bodhisattva asked his question in verse:

"World-honored One with all the wonderful signs,   147
Let me now ask about him once more:
For what reason is this son of the Buddha
Named 'Observing the Sounds of the World'?"
World-honored One with all the wonderful signs
Answered Aksayamati in verse:
"You listen now to the practice of Avalokitesvara,   149
Who well responds to every region.
His great vow is as deep as the sea,
Inconceivable even after many kalpas.
Having served Buddhas in the hundreds of billions,
He has made a great and pure vow.
Let me briefly tell you: 152
Hearing his name and seeing his form,
Keeping him unremittingly in mind,
Can eliminate all manner of suffering.
Suppose someone with harmful intent,   155
Casts you into a great pit of fire;
Keep in mind Avalokitesvara's powers,
And the pit of fire will change into a pond.
Or you are cast adrift upon an immense ocean,
Menaced by dragons, fish, and demons;

Keep in mind Avalokitesvara's powers,
And the waves will not drown you.

156   Or someone pushes you down,
From the top of Mount Sumeru;
Keep in mind Avalokitesvara's powers,
And you will hang in the sky like the sun.
Or you are pursued by evil doers,
Who push you down from Mount Vajra;
Keep in mind Avalokitesvara's powers,
And not one of your hairs will be harmed.

158   Or if surrounded by malevolent brigands,
Each one brandishing a knife to attack you;
Keep in mind Avalokitesvara's powers,
And they will all experience a sense of compassion.
Or if persecuted by the royal court,
Facing death by execution;
Keep in mind Avalokitesvara's powers,
And the executioner's blade will break into pieces.

160   Or if imprisoned with cangue and chains,
Hands and feet manacled and shackled;
Keep in mind Avalokitesvara's powers,
And the bonds will loosen and you will be liberated.
If there is someone who would do you harm,
Using spells and various poisons;
Keep in mind Avalokitesvara's powers,
And any harm will rebound on the originator.

162   Or if you encounter evil *raksas*,
Venomous dragons, various ghosts, and the like;
Keep in mind Avalokitesvara's powers,
And then none of them will dare harm you.

If you are surrounded by evil beasts
With their sharp teeth and claws so horrifying;
Keep in mind Avalokitesvara's powers,
And they will flee in all directions.
When lizards, snakes, vipers, and scorpions
Scorch you with their poisonous vapors;
Keep in mind Avalokitesvara's powers,
And they will retreat at the sound of your voice.
When thunderclouds rumble with lighting strikes,
As hailstones and torrential rains come down;
Keep in mind Avalokitesvara's powers,
And the storm will disperse that very moment.
Living beings suffer in agony,   164
Oppressed by immeasurable pain;
The power of Avalokitesvara's wondrous wisdom
Can bring liberation from the world's sufferings.
Perfect in supernatural powers,   167
Widely practicing the skillful means of wisdom,
In all the lands of the ten directions,
There is no place where he fails to manifest.
The lower realms in all their forms,
That of hell-beings, hungry ghosts, and animals,
The sufferings of birth, old age, sickness, and death,
He steadily brings them all to an end.
Contemplation of truth, contemplation of purity,   169
Contemplation of the vast and greater wisdom,
Contemplation of compassion
     and contemplation of kindness;
Ever longed for, ever looked up to.

His undefiled light of purity
Is the wisdom-sun dispelling all darkness,
What can quell winds and fires that bring disaster
And illuminate the world universally.
175   Precepts of his compassionate body
            are like rolling thunder;
The profundity of his kind mind is like a great cloud;
He showers us with Dharma rain like nectar,
That extinguishes the flames of affliction.
176   When lawsuits bring you to court,
Or when fear strikes you in battle,
Keep in mind Avalokitesvara's powers,
And the enemy forces will all retreat.
177   Contemplating the world's voices with a wondrous voice,
A Brahma voice, an ocean-tide voice,
What surpasses those voices of the world;
Therefore constantly keep them in mind.
179   Never doubt from moment to moment,
The pure and noble Avalokitesvara;
For those in pain and agony, or facing death,
He can be their aid and support!
180   In possession of all merit and virtue,
He views living beings with compassionate eyes;
His ocean of accumulated merit is infinite,
So worship him with prostrations.

185   At this time Dharanimdhara Bodhisattva rose from his seat, came forward, and said to the Buddha, "World-honored One, if there are living beings who hear this chapter on Avalokitesvara Bodhisattva about his freedom of action, his revelation of the

universal gate, and his supernatural powers, it should be known that their merits are not few."

When the Buddha preached this chapter on the Universal Gate, 187 the eighty-four thousand living beings assembled there all generated the aspiration to attain *anuttara-samyak-sambodhi.*

I

Question and Answer

Though the entirety of the *Universal Gate Sutra* details the belief in Avalokitesvara Bodhisattva, it can be divided into two major sections: narrative text and laudatory verse. The narrative text, which is placed at the beginning of the chapter, is in prose while the laudatory verse, which occurs after the narrative text, repeats the main points of the narrative in verse form. Due to the repetition, the main points of the *Universal Gate Sutra* are contained completely in the narrative text section.

The narrative text is a dialog between Sakyamuni Buddha and the assembly, and can be further divided into two sections based on the two questions asked by Aksayamati Bodhisattva: How did Avalokitesvara Bodhisattva get his name, and what skillful means does he employ to teach the Dharma.

Aside from the two sections of narrative text and laudatory verse, and apart from the two questions of Aksayamati Bodhisattva, the place to start an examination of the sutra is with the chapter's very first words: "at that time." What time does this refer to?

Zhili gives a very matter of fact explanation in his *Notes on the Meaning of Avalokitesvara*: "at that time," he states, simply refers to the time after the previous chapter of the *Lotus Sutra* ends and before the Universal Gate chapter begins. Another explanation states that the time mentioned at the outset of the chapter is significant because, having heard the previous chapter, the Gadgadasvara Bodhisattva chapter, the assembly became ecstatic and hoped to hear of Avalo-kitesvara's vow to inspire wholesomeness in all living beings.

Though the time mentioned within "at that time" refers to the Universal Gate chapter's place within the *Lotus Sutra*, when the Universal Gate chapter is recited as a separate text, it allows us to think outside this classification. From the perspective of the Buddha, "at that time" simply refers to the time when the Buddha deemed it right to deliver the teachings contained in the Universal Gate chapter. From the perspective of living beings, "at that time" refers to when the proper causes and conditions are present to allow them to listen to the teachings. When viewed this way the opening words of "at that time" need not apply to only a specific time, but can be any time when these factors are present, even today. "At that time" is limitless.

Aksayamati Bodhisattva

The interlocutor of the *Universal Gate Sutra* is Aksayamati Bodhisattva. Aksayamati Bodhisattva is said to be the successor of Samantabhadra Buddha, who presides over the Eastern Realm of Watchfulness. In the Realm of Watchfulness, there are only bodhisattvas, no *sravakas* or *pratyekabuddhas*. Typically, Aksayamati Bodhisattva assists Samantabhadra Buddha in teaching the Dharma, but for the occasion of Sakyamuni Buddha's lotus assembly, he has been summoned to visit Vulture Peak in the Saha World and assist Sakyamuni Buddha.

The fact that Aksayamati Bodhisattva asked about Avalokitesvara Bodhisattva is highly significant. Aksayamati Bodhisattva's Chinese name is *wujin yi* (無盡意), meaning "infinite intention," and refers to the bodhisattva's boundless intention to liberate beings. There are infinite worlds with infinite living beings generating infinite karma. Many do not understand that all phenomena are illusory, as they arise from differing causes and conditions, and instead cling to them as if they exist. Such is the unenlightened state of ordinary beings.

To put forth the view that everything is empty because it is a compound of causes and conditions is the Hinayana or the provisional Mahayana view. The absolute Mahayana view is neither predisposed towards existence with its many distinctions nor the oneness of emptiness. The absolute Mahayana view considers all things with their infinite interactions to be the true reality of all phenomena, and that all phenomena in the world benefit one another by mutually bestowing blessings upon one another. This is a bodhisattva's vow and practice.

The *sravakas* or *pratyekabuddhas* who practice for their own benefit do not understand the principle of mutual blessings. Thus Aksayamati Bodhisattva's infinite intention to compassionately liberate infinite beings encompasses the essence of Mahayana Buddhism. Indeed, it is profound that such a bodhisattva would pose a question about Avalokitesvara Bodhisattva, whose name is heard in all directions, and whose prestige places him among the sages, for Avalokitesvara Bodhisattva's compassion as described in the *Universal Gate Sutra* also depicts this sense of "infinite."

The Method of Asking

Aksayamati Bodhisattva rose from his seat, bared his right shoulder, [and] put his palms together facing the Buddha....

There are also many interesting details contained within the language of how Aksayamati Bodhisattva asks his question. Concerning rising from his seat, Zhizhe's *Interpretation on Mind Contemplation* offers a deep analysis:

> Emptiness itself is the seat, and as this emptiness
> has no attachments, therefore it is called "rising."

Aksayamati Bodhisattva takes the emptiness of all phenomena as his "seat," or foundation. He has turned away from the duality of emptiness and existence and attained the true wisdom of the Middle Way, and also abides without attachment. This realization of the emptiness of all phenomena is the gateway through which equality is established. Aksayamati Bodhisattva thus rises from this domain, requested by Samantabhadra Buddha, and appears at Sakyamuni Buddha's lotus assembly to ask the right question in accordance with the faculties of the audience. Thus, by "rising" from the seat of emptiness, he manifests in the assembly, amid the fate of existence and distinctions, to teach living beings.

The mention that Aksayamati Bodhisattva "bared his right shoulder" is a reference to how a Buddhist monastic robe is worn. In India, the robe was worn with the left shoulder covered and the right shoulder exposed as a convenience when working and as a way of showing respect when doing something on behalf of one's teacher. When venerating Buddhas and bodhisattvas, we emulate the cultural aspects of the Indian practice of baring the right shoulder.

Concerning the right shoulder, Zhizhe describes the left and right shoulders in *Interpretation on Mind Contemplation* as representing relative and absolute truth. The left shoulder represents the absolute truth of emptiness, and as it cannot be expressed, the shoulder is covered. The right shoulder represents the relative or provisional truth of skillful means, and is thus exposed. Another way the two are explained is that the left shoulder represents meditative concentration while the right shoulder represents wisdom, thus the act of exposing the right shoulder is to rise out of meditative concentration to emit the light of wisdom.

The gesture of placing the palms together mentioned in the text is also an Indian gesture of respect towards superiors where both palms and all ten fingers are joined together. Symbolically the gesture of joining palms is explained as the ten fingers of the hands representing the ten realms, and that joining them together is symbolic of the oneness of the ten realms. The gesture of joining palms also shows the non-duality of living beings and the Buddha, as well as of ignorance and enlightenment.

The Question

World-honored One, for what reason is Avalokitesvara Bodhisattva named "Observing the Sounds of the World"?

Aksayamati's question itself does not require any special explanation, but it would be useful to examine the name used to address

the Buddha, "World-honored One." Sakyamuni Buddha is known
as the teacher of the three realms* and the compassionate father of
all beings. He is honored throughout the mundane and supramundane realms, and is thus known as the "World-honored One." There
are ten epithets that are usually used to describe the Buddha, with
"World-honored One" simply being the most prevalent. The ten
epithets of the Buddha are:

Chinese	English
如來	Thus Come (*tathagata*)
應供	Worthy One (*arhat*)
正徧知	Truly All-Knowing
明行足	Perfect in Knowledge and Conduct
善逝	Well-Gone
世間解	Knower of the World
無上士	Unsurpassed
調御丈夫	Tamer
天人師	Teacher of Celestial and Human Beings
佛	Enlightened One (*buddha*)

The Answer

**The Buddha answered Aksayamati Bodhisattva,
"Good men, if there be countless hundreds of millions of billions of living beings experiencing all**

---

*. The three realms are not distinct from the ten realms mentioned earlier;
they are just a different way of describing the multitude of worlds in Buddhist
cosmology. *Ed.*

**manner of suffering who hear of Avalokitesvara
Bodhisattva and call his name with single-minded
effort, then Avalokitesvara Bodhisattva will instantly observe the sound of their cries, and they
will all be liberated.**

This first passage outlines Sakyamuni Buddha's teachings in
the *Universal Gate Sutra*. This passage succinctly describes
Avalokitesvara Bodhisattva's vow and compassion, how living
beings can call upon him, and the benefits of doing so. This passage is the most important in the sutra, and as previously mentioned, is the textual basis for Kumarajiva's Chinese translation
of Avalokitesvara's name. However, before a full examination of
the ideas in this passage, it is necessary to explain some terminol-
ogy, specifically the Buddhist understanding of "living beings" and
"suffering."

The Sanskrit word on which the Chinese translations are based
is *sattva*, signifying all organisms. One Chinese translation of this
word is *zhongsheng* (眾生), "many beings." The meaning of this
particular translation is appropriate for three reasons:

1. Such beings are born into this world with many others.
2. Such beings are born into the world from a combination of
   many causes and conditions.
3. Such beings are born in many places.

Xuanzang later proposed a new translation: *youqing* (有情),
"having sentience," or "sentient beings." This translation's emphasis
on sentience draws a sharper contrast dividing *sattva* from inani-
mate objects.

The passage mentions "countless hundreds of millions of billions of living beings," necessarily including those beings in hell, the realm of hungry ghosts, the animal realm, and the realm of *asuras*. The living beings of these four lower realms of rebirth who experience suffering are truly countless. However, all of the Buddha's teachings focus on the human world, why then the mention of non-human beings to be liberated?

Avalokitesvara Bodhisattva is known as the great liberator of the Saha World, yet the beings mentioned above do appear in the human realm. As mentioned before, a person in the human realm generates these other realms in their mind every day: the anger of hell, the greed of the realm of hungry ghosts, and the wild, perverse mind of the animal realm. The beings of these realms of suffering do indeed exist in this human realm.

"All manner of suffering" mentioned in Sakyamuni Buddha's response is elaborated upon and made more specific later on in the sutra, but in a general sense it can refer to the eight kinds of suffering mentioned throughout the Buddhist sutras: birth, aging, sickness, death, affliction, sorrow, being near those we hate, being separate from those we love, and not getting what we want. Each of these types of suffering is like the suffering of hell, the realm of hungry ghosts, the animal realm, and the *asura* realm as experienced within the mind. However, a careful consideration of the source of all these types of suffering would show that they are all generated by the desire for survival. There is no desire more formidable and intense than the human drive for survival, and so this desire is the origin from which all the various kinds of suffering arise.

Sound and Hearing

The faculty of hearing features prominently in the description of Avalokitesvara Bodhisattva. The character *wen* (聞), "hear" is used to describe those who have knowledge of Avalokitesvara: they have heard his name, know who he is, and thus *cheng* (稱), "call" to him. Avalokitesvara Bodhisattva hears the sound of their cries and is then able to liberate them from suffering. The text's use of "hear" is quite profound. Hearing encompasses the mutual interaction of perception and response, and the text shows the bodhisattva and living beings both listening and responding to one another.

Ears themselves are quite special, and are what allow the bodhisattvas and living beings to mutually perceive and respond to one another. The *Suramgama Sutra* describes three special attributes of hearing:

1. **True Perception:** While the eyes can be blocked and things concealed from our vision, the ears can hear sounds even miles away.
2. **True Completeness:** The eyes are only capable of seeing what is directly in front of them, while the ears can hear regardless of whether sounds are coming in front, in back, to the left, or to the right.
3. **True Continuity:** Our sense of hearing allows us to pass on what has happened in the past to the present, and what is happening now to the future.

Sound and hearing is the major vehicle by which living beings in the Saha World are liberated from their suffering, which is why Avalokitesvara Bodhisattva is regarded as a great liberator of human beings.

The text describes the manner that people call out to Avalokitesvara Bodhisattva as "with single-minded effort." What exactly does this mean? In Chinese the expression is *yixin* (一心), "one mind," which means to maintain only one thought in the mind. Thus, "single-minded effort" means to think of Avalokitesvara Bodhisattva with every thought and not to allow any other thoughts to intrude.

The entreaty to "call his name" traditionally means to recite "I take refuge in the great, compassionate Avalokitesvara Bodhisattva," the Chinese of which is provided below:

南	無	大	悲	觀	世	音	菩	薩
na	*mo*	*da*	*bei*	*guan*	*shi*	*yin*	*pu*	*sa*

"I take refuge in the great, compassionate Avalokitesvara Bodhisattva"

That being said, the most important component of calling Avalokitesvara Bodhisattva's name is not in the words, but in the mind. Mindful recitation of the name should be our foundation. We should constantly recite "I take refuge in the great, compassionate Avalokitesvara Bodhisattva" until there is no longer any distinction between Avalokitesvara and ourselves: you are Avalokitesvara and Avalokitesvara is you, such that you recite the name effortlessly. This is what calling the name really sounds like.

There are some who will say that, when calling Avalokitesvara's name, it is only necessary to do so mentally, and that one need not actually make a sound, but such an approach misses the point. There are also those who say, "There is no need to actually seek help from the bodhisattvas; for as long as you are sincere the bodhisattvas will protect you." This too is mistaken, but in the very least it is a good admonition to those who recite the name perfunctorily and lack sincerity.

Fundamentally, the body and mind are one, and any internal sincerity would also appear outwardly. If someone were truly operating with single-minded effort, they would surely make a sound as they call the name. It is only natural, and to do so is the true meaning of calling the name. Moreover, the deeper the sincerity of the person calling Avalokitesvara's name, the more fully that person will experience the bodhisattva's great compassion in response. When such a level of sincerity is reached, you will unconsciously utter sounds of gratitude even if someone tells you to stop. It is just as if the weather were bitterly cold or burning hot and one says, even without meaning to, "It's so cold!" or "It's so hot!"

Having heard the name of the noble Avalokitesvara Bodhisattva, you can recite it and Avalokitesvara will hear your single-minded request and bestow his aid. This is what it means to perfect the sense of hearing. One cannot truly understand what is meant by "hear" in this instance without reciting the name.

The Self

If one were to thoughtfully consider the notion of "single-minded effort," one would realize that before it can really be accomplished, one must have an intimate understanding of oneself. The problems of the world or the universe that Buddhism addresses are secondary or tertiary concerns. To learn Buddhism means to learn about oneself; the questions one must ask must be asked of oneself alone. The primary question, simply stated, is What kind of "self" should one be? Even if one were to give this question careful consideration, it would be impossible to come up with a definitive answer.

Still, that does not mean that we can do nothing; it is at times like this that our inherent mind appears.

The Buddhist text the *Treatise on Awakening of Faith in Mahayana* describes the liberation of the self from two aspects. The first states that true reality already exists just as it is, but is obscured by ignorance. The method for removing ignorance is called "the dependent origination of suchness." The other aspect begins with ignorance as its basis, and prescribes various types of learning to become less ignorant; this is called the "dependent origination of ignorance." Such expansive and philosophical texts like the *Awakening of Faith* or the *Treatise on Consciousness Only* do not address the problems of the universe, but rather are concerned with the self. The problem of ignorance mentioned in the *Awakening of Faith,* as well as the *alaya* consciousness mentioned in the *Treatise on Consciousness Only,* are different names for the "self" which exist in our minds. To be liberated we must use skillful means to remove our attachments to the sense of self.

There is no purpose to Sakyamuni Buddha's forty-nine years of teaching, the twelve divisions of the Buddhist canon or the efforts of generations of teachers and patriarchs other than addressing the problem of the self. This is what the *Universal Gate Sutra* is all about—liberating the "self" of all beings. There is nothing else.

Attachment

One may ask: If desire is indeed the source of all suffering, where does this desire come from? The answer is simple and definite: desire comes from the existence of a self. Through our ignorance we are attached to the self, and our attachment and desire for phenomena is generated from the sense of ownership that comes from our attachment to the self. Because of the attachment to the self and phenomena, we experience all kinds of suffering and create all kinds of unwholesomeness.

The people of this world are as illusory as the moon reflected in water or a performance upon a stage. The self is not real. But we fill ourselves with greed, anger, and wickedness such that we cannot easily see ourselves. To be able to see what is real, we must reflect upon the self using the mirror of great compassion. This is what is true; such a mirror is nothing other than the constant mindfulness of the name and compassionate visage of Avalokitesvara Bodhisattva.

Our attachment to the self and phenomena is actually a manifestation of our ignorance and suffering from the karma we have incurred since beginningless time. The need to purify oneself, eliminate attachment, and end the cycle of birth and death is not readily apparent to ordinary, worldly people. There is only one time when we can really understand why this is so important, and that is when we have become purified, ended the cycle of birth and death, and attained *nirvana*.

Knowing we are about to die and staring directly at death can be the most sacred and genuine moment of all. It is often said that people truly speak from the heart when death draws near. Even if someone were guilty of the most heinous crimes, he can still change at the moment of death.

We need not curse death, for death spares no one. With life, there must be death. The cycle of birth and death is part of reality. The question is not whether or not we will die, but whether we can maintain our faith at the time of death. As long as we have faith, what is there to fear from death?

Death is the end of life, like a bomb exploding with a bang. At that time there is nothing worth hanging on to, for nothing holds any value. All the wealth in the world no longer has any significance. If you think about it, death is quite a lonely affair, for the only thing we bring with us is a lifetime of positive and negative karma. There is nothing else we can take with us.

In life, we experience all kinds of desire and suffering produced by our attachment to the self and phenomena, but when death approaches, none of what we have become so attached to belongs to us anyway. From this perspective, what is the point of grasping at things when we are alive, especially with all the unnecessary suffering it entails?

Liberation

Sakyamuni Buddha says that "Avalokitesvara Bodhisattva will instantly observe the sound of their cries and they will all be liberated." But what is it that they are being liberated from? Such beings are liberated from all suffering.

The liberation mentioned in the sutra is not the same as being relieved of a physical burden. Instead it is the liberation which comes from our single-minded effort in calling the name of Avalokitesvara Bodhisattva. This kind of liberation is created by combining the three types of karma: mental karma by cultivating a mind of true devotion, verbal karma by reciting the name, and bodily karma by joining one's palms together. When the three kinds of karma are combined, our efforts to single-mindedly call the name of Avalokitesvara will liberate us in two ways.

First, by single-mindedly calling the name of Avalokitesvara Bodhisattva, we will be supported by the light of his compassion. Our minds and bodies will turn away from the sources of our suffering, ignorance, and negative karma. When our lives are imbued with such pure faith we will be able to act with good conduct.

Secondly, by single-mindedly calling the name of Avalokitesvara Bodhisattva with utmost sincerity, we can be assured that our pleas will be heard. Though physically suffering within the cycle of birth and death, a person who has faith that Avalokitesvara will respond will not feel that their suffering is suffering, and thus will be liberated from suffering.

Avalokitesvara's merit and virtue are truly great. Though our days are spent entangled in suffering and affliction that we cannot get away from, we need only rely upon single-mindedly calling the name of Avalokitesvara Bodhisattva. This is the way that this practice reaches fruition; the way that it can liberate us is by giving us the ability to endure amid all such suffering and affliction.

The liberation, perfect perception, and single-minded calling of Avalokitesvara Bodhisattva cannot be explained in theoretical terms alone. Each of us must bring our body, speech, and mind together. When the three types of karma are combined and we single-mindedly call the bodhisattva's name, then naturally we will be liberated through Avalokitesvara Bodhisattva's perfect perception. If we wish to be joyful and happy in body and mind, we must single-mindedly call the name of Avalokitesvara.

Having discussed all this, most people will still feel that such a thing is not easy to do. We bind ourselves down with layer upon layer of the chains of attachment and affliction. We have no freedom at all, and therefore we suffer. But the things that bind us do not come from outside; it is we who bind ourselves.

Once someone asked a monk, "Oh monk, please tell me how to practice to liberate myself."

"Who has bound you?" the monk asked in reply.

From such a counter-question we can see that no one else has put us into bondage. We each tie ourselves up with our own rope.

But, once we know this, we can free ourselves by applying the mind of compassion—such is as if Avalokitesvara himself appeared before us and liberated us. By ridding the mind of the attachment to self, we will see ourselves and others as equal, and directly understand the adage, "I am all living beings and all living beings are me." With such a state of compassion, we truly free ourselves from the filth and mire of delusion and purify our minds.

At this point the mind of Avalokitesvara and our own become one, and we are naturally freed from the suffering of attachment to the self and delusion. When the mind is purified in such a way, we can then engage in things single-mindedly. Such a mind is unified and without duality, with only pure thoughts and no delusions. This state of mind comes from single-mindedly calling the name of Avalokitesvara Bodhisattva and receiving the liberation Avalokitesvara gives you.

II

The Seven Calamities

With this passage Sakyamuni Buddha begins to explain specific ways that Avalokitesvara Bodhisattva is capable of interceding. The first group consists of seven different dangers, together known as the "seven calamities." They are fire, flood, wind storms, weapons, evil spirits, imprisonment, and brigands.

The Calamity of Fire

If anyone who upholds the name of Avalokitesvara Bodhisattva were to fall into a great fire, the fire would be unable to burn that person due to the bodhisattva's awe-inspiring spiritual powers.

According to the passage, if someone who holds firmly to the name of Avalokitesvara were to find themselves in a fire, no matter how big, they need not fear being burned by it because of the bodhisattva's awe-inspiring spiritual powers.

Specifically the passage describes one who "upholds the name." The Chinese character *chi* (持), "uphold," means to hold firmly to or

51

mindfully maintain something. One who upholds the name recites it single-mindedly and with devout reverence. If we hope to escape from any sort of calamity, then we must believe in Avalokitesvara Bodhisattva, his spiritual powers, and his merit. Without such faith, it is hard to obtain the bodhisattva's intercession.

The seven calamities each describe external dangers, but these dangers also occur in our minds. For example, the calamity of fire can be likened to the fire of anger. The *Sutra of the Teachings Bequeathed by the Buddha* states:

> As for the harm done by anger, it can destroy all positive karma and ruin one's good reputation. People will turn away from you in this life and in future lives. Clearly understand that the mind of anger is worse than a fierce fire. Always be on guard against it and do not let it in.

Anger is like an uncontrollable fire being carried by a fierce wind. In the same way, the *Lotus Sutra* likens the world to a burning house, caught in the fires of our afflictions. The fires of anger do not lie outside, but are within the mind. At their most severe, anger and hatred can provoke hostility towards others, and acting on this hostility can lead us to do harm. Not only is this morally wrong, but it is spiritually damaging. The harm done by anger can destroy all the roots of goodness.

Where do these fires come from? They arise from the attachment to the self, seeking benefit for ourselves, and having pride in ourselves. Someone once asked the famous Chan master Bankei, "I'm bad-tempered by nature and easily become angered. There's nothing I can do about it. Can't you please do something to cure me of this?"

"Oh, this illness is very strange," Bankei replied. "To be bad-tempered by nature is even more interesting. This old monk has never seen what a bad temperament is like. Why don't you take it out and show it to me?"

"Venerable, that's impossible! How can I possibly take it out?"

"See? I tell you to take it out but you cannot do so. Clearly this is not some inherent flaw, but arises from anger and hatred."

This reply stunned the questioner, and his bad temperament never returned.

Fires, floods, and other calamities are not limited to the tangible and the visible. They can also be like the fires of anger that can burn within our breast when we are insulted and humiliated by others. When insulted, if someone were to shout back with an even louder voice, would the angry expression on that person's face not resemble a blazing fire?

There is an old Buddhist saying, "The fires of anger can burn up a forest of merit." Only when the fires of anger are smothered can we appreciate things like reason and human emotion that come from a mind that is calm and tranquil. As long as we can restrain thoughts of anger, then we can maintain an unperturbed and tranquil attitude no matter what setbacks appear to trouble us. In this way we can transcend any concern over praise or blame, and reach a state described by the Chinese poet Su Shi as "remaining unmoved by the influence of the eight winds."

Suppose someone were to criticize you and you became angry. If the person is a person of integrity and good character and is criticizing your behavior, then you are likely in the wrong. But even if you are being criticized by a person of ignoble character, in getting angry at that person you set yourself on equal footing with him, and if you were to respond back you would place yourself even lower. Therefore, when a person of integrity criticizes us, we should examine ourselves to see where our errors lie, but when some ignoble individual criticizes us, we should not go down to their level or take it so seriously.

Most people understand this in principle, but we still find it hard to practice. Even the minor affairs of daily life, like someone gossiping at our expense, are enough to stir the mind to unwitting anger. Once the flames of anger are unleashed, we might just destroy even the things we hold dear. Indeed, the human mind is truly like the burning house of the *Lotus Sutra*.

When we don't get what we want, the flames of anger and hatred blaze because of the fiery desires of the human heart. The inability to do as we wish is common in this world, and the only way we will be able to extinguish the fires within the mind is to douse them with the water of wisdom.

The world is not a place where our wishes can be fulfilled. Our wishes can only be fulfilled within the mind. But even though this is true, we are still sometimes dissatisfied because we handle things unskillfully. This is the dissatisfaction that leads us to suffer.

If we were to investigate the cause of this, we can see that it stems from a failure to cultivate real wisdom. Without sufficient wisdom, we develop many ways of seeing any given thing: we want to do something a certain way, but also want to do it other ways. The light of wisdom within the mind becomes obscured, and we become confused and miserable.

Although there are myriad phenomena in the universe, each with their own distinctive features, they share the same source. If we can restore the mind to its original state of calm, serenity, and absolute equality, then neither life nor death, neither happiness nor suffering, neither satisfaction nor dissatisfaction, nor anything else will be able to throw our minds into disorder. Even the phenomena of the universe in all their variation would be unable to confuse us. If we can accomplish this, then we have already attained great wisdom. This great wisdom will grant us the courage to endure any praise or blame, and develop the compassionate sense of equality that is beneficial to all.

Not only is Avalokitesvara Bodhisattva a manifestation of great compassion but also through his compassion to liberate living beings a being of great wisdom and great courage. By making the mind like the mind of Avalokitesvara Bodhisattva and having the great compassion to liberate living beings, we can also participate in Avalokitesvara's spiritual powers. When we have attained this state, we, too, can fall into a fire and not be burned.

When the fires of anger are about to burn our mind and body, if we single-mindedly call the name of Avalokitesvara Bodhisattva, we will be spared from such a fiery calamity. Is this not an example of Avalokitesvara's awe-inspiring spiritual powers? But even so, these powers are simply the powers of great compassion, great wisdom, and great courage. When the fires of anger are raging in our breast, if we single-mindedly call his name, Avalokitesvara Bodhisattva will transform into the water of compassion and extinguish the flames.

The Calamity of Flood

If anyone, carried away by a flood, were to call his name, that person would immediately reach a shallow place.

This is the second of the seven calamities, the calamity of flood. From a psychological perspective, we are swept into the sea of life and death where we float around aimlessly, craving life and dreading death. This is the human condition. We are prone to being led astray into the waters of desire, sinking deeper and deeper. There is no telling how many people have brought shame and disgrace upon themselves because they were tempted by their desires. The *Sutra in Forty-two Sections* states:

> People who harbor love and desire do not perceive the Way. They are like clear water that has been stirred up by the hand; though many people gather around it, none will see their reflections in it. People who become entangled with love and desire stir up impurities within the mind, and so fail to perceive the Way. You practitioners should abandon love and desire. Once the impurity of love and desire has been cleared away, then one will be able to perceive the Way! What makes people ignorant and muddled are love and desire.

For ages, countless people have been led astray by love and desire. Many have been unable to make any progress because of these two emotions, while some have even destroyed their lives and families. Where do love and desire come from? We know that anger arises from unhappiness; conversely love and desire arise out of happiness. One example is a person who acts irrationally for a boyfriend or girlfriend whom they love deeply. Such an individual brushes aside the opinions of parents and the pleas of friends.

Many young men and women ignore their careers and disregard their futures for the sake of love.

People who are swept up in the vortex of love and desire with such abandon do so mainly because of an unyielding sense of love for themselves. If such people could step back from their own self-love a bit and cultivate the compassionate mind of Avalokitesvara, then naturally they would not allow anything bad to happen to others caused by their own love and desire. Avalokitesvara only wishes for all living beings to be free from suffering and does not care for his own safety and happiness.

Such things are easy to say, for even if we know we are floating aimlessly in the sea of love and desire and have already reached the point where we are drowning, we still cling to our sense of self. We do this without even realizing it or trying to change. How sad indeed!

If in these times we think of Avalokitesvara's universal compassion and discard our own greed and longing, then our mind can become as clear as a mirror. With great wisdom we will be able to know all phenomena without becoming attached to them, and possess the great courage to remove the attachments of love.

In principle, there would no longer be any distinction between loving and not loving, for everything would be equal. There would be no concept of beauty or ugliness, nor any difference between love and hate. Then we could remove the root cause of the cycle of birth and death: desire. Equipped with the merit of calling the name of Avalokitesvara Bodhisattva, we will surely find a shallow place of safety amidst the billowing waves of love and desire.

The Calamity of Wind Storms

> If there are living beings in the hundreds of mil-
> lions of billions who go out to sea in search of such
> treasures as gold, silver, lapis lazuli, mother of
> pearl, carnelian, coral, amber, and pearls, and if a
> fierce storm were to blow their ship off course to
> make landfall in the territory of *raksas,* and further
> if among them there is even one person who calls
> the name of Avalokitesvara Bodhisattva, then all
> of those people will be liberated from the torment
> of the *raksas.* This is why the bodhisattva is named
> "Observing the Sounds of the World."

This passage covers the third of the seven calamities: the calamity
of wind storms, which is also sometimes called the calamity of *raksas. Raksa* is a Sanskrit word which refers to a specific type of malevolent supernatural being that eats humans. The expression used
for "ship" in this passage, *chuanfang* (船舫), specifically refers to a
lavish boat with two hulls, resembling a catamaran. This serves as
a metaphor for how the human being is a union of the mind and
body. The treasures mentioned in the passage are manifold, but
they are all simply rare and valuable things.

Though the treasures mentioned in the sutra are specific precious materials, they can also refer to spiritual wealth, of which
there are seven kinds:

1. The Wealth of Faith

Several Buddhist sutras mention the importance of faith. The
Treatise on the Perfection of Great Wisdom states: "Only faith

allows one to enter the great ocean of the Dharma." The *Flower Adornment Sutra* states: "Faith is the mother of merit leading to the source of enlightenment." If someone trying to learn Buddhism lacks devout faith, they cannot possible enter the Dharma. If they have doubts instead of faith, they will experience worry and distress and lose sight of the path they should be practicing. When it comes to Buddhist practice, being even a hairbreadth away from the correct path can lead you away by thousands of miles. One thought of devout faith is more valuable than anything. If the mind is doubtful, not only can we not have faith but we may even generate unwholesome thoughts in its place, and the results of our previous efforts will be lost. Cultivating faith is the best method for removing doubt and delusion. For this reason we should each maintain a faith that is diamond-like in its indestructibility.

2. The Wealth of Diligence

Diligence means endeavoring to improve with vigorous effort. If we do not understand the value of diligence, even the best religion will have nothing to offer us. There is an old Chinese saying, "There is something gained with each drop of sweat." Without diligence, we cannot experience the real flavor of the Dharma.

3. The Wealth of Morality

Morality means not doing what is wrong. This can be accomplished by strictly adhering to the precepts as the Buddha instructed and not breaking them in any way. Maintaining proper conduct and observing rules both mundane and supramundane is the wealth of morality. Having complete disregard for the precepts is undisciplined self-indulgence, and naturally leads to corruption and improper behavior.

4. The Wealth of Listening

Listening is the first step towards knowledge. If human beings do not seek knowledge and fail to receive instruction, they are no different from animals. Only by listening to the teachings can we understand the truth. No one has ever entered the path without listening to the teachings. We should listen to the teachings with a sense of humility, for a humble person has emptied the self. This is a prerequisite for listening to the teachings and the beginning of the spiritual path. Having listened to the teachings, they must then be put into practice to gain any real benefits. In this way listening leads to thinking, and thinking leads to practice.

5. The Wealth of Giving

If we are trying to practice the Buddhist ideal of compassion, giving is most important. If we hope that we might gain something from our acts of generosity, then we are taking, not giving. Taking is the opposite of giving, and yet another form of attachment. When we give we should be like the rays of the sun: shining down equally upon all things on earth. A bodhisattva must possess the four immeasurable minds: loving-kindness, compassion, joy, and equanimity. He should have loving-kindness that shares in joy, and immeasurable compassion that shares in suffering. When performing acts of compassion, we should understand that other people are neither telling nor forcing us to do so. Rather, we should be happy to do so, for giving brings immeasurable joy. If we try to share joy or alleviate suffering with a sense of unwillingness or discontent, this is not compassion. Only by giving with no expectation of reward and with immeasurable loving-kindness, compassion, and joy can we achieve immeasurable equanimity.

6. The Wealth of Wisdom

Wisdom is meditation applied; thus the wealth of wisdom can also be called the wealth of wisdom and meditation. Meditation is stopping delusion, and wisdom is seeing the mind. Meditation collects one's thoughts and prevents distracting, delusional thoughts, while wisdom illuminates all phenomena and brings an end to wrong views. We use wisdom as we use our eyes when walking: without wisdom, we would be blind and wander in whatever direction we were headed. The *Treatise on the Perfection of Great Wisdom* says concerning cultivation, "eyes for wisdom and feet for practice." Without practice we cannot move forward, and without wisdom we cannot see. We must have both to get to where we are going. Even if we possess the wealth of diligence, the wealth of morality, and the wealth of giving, without the wealth of wisdom we cannot advance.

7. The Wealth of Conscience

Conscience means to feel ashamed and humble for doing something wrong. The *Treatise on the Mahayana Abhidharma* explains it this way:

> Conscience is to feel shame towards all wrongdoing that originates from oneself. Humility is to feel shame towards all wrongdoing that originates from others.

One cannot enter the spiritual path without conscience. The *Sutra of Teachings Bequeathed by the Buddha* states: "Being clothed with a sense of shame is the foremost adornment." There is nothing finer and more beautiful than feeling a sense of shame. To generate this state of mind is truly gratifying. With a sense of shame in doing wrong we can generate respect and a sense of propriety, which will be followed by a sense of faith. It is really a pity to be a human being and yet be unable to feel a sense of shame for doing something wrong. Shame is aligned with Buddha nature, for only by having a sense of shame can we realistically put wisdom, faith, and morality into practice.

These are known as the "seven aspects of noble wealth," and they are variously explained throughout the Buddhist scriptures. If you are in pursuit of these treasures without a firm and unmoving mind, you may find yourself blown off course by the winds of affliction and ignorance, thinking "I have been tricked! What is the point of learning Buddhism anyway? Even if I were to practice, it would be no use."

Once doubt has taken the place of faith, we lose our diligence and break moral precepts. This leads to all sorts of foolish and unruly behavior. As a result, we take rather than give, become ignorant instead of wise, and forego shame for shamelessness. The mind which could have entered the path to enlightenment is cast into the perilous sea and drifts to the land of *raksas*.

When we find ourselves in the territory of *raksas* amid the waves of greed, anger, and ignorance, if we think, "I take refuge in Avalokitesvara Bodhisattva," and have thoughts of universal compassion then the fierce winds which beset us will cease and the waves will subside.

The Calamity of Weapons

**Or if someone facing imminent attack calls the name
of Avalokitesvara Bodhisattva, the knives and clubs**

held by the attackers will then break into pieces, and that person will attain liberation.

The fourth calamity is the calamity of weapons. The knives and clubs mentioned in the passage are not only physical weapons but also refer to the harm that arrogance and anger do to others. Arrogance is like a knife: we think and speak highly of ourselves and denigrate others, unwittingly becoming jealous towards those who are better than ourselves. Anger is like a club: it is the furious face and wrathful mind with which we bludgeon others.

When we ourselves are persecuted by such attitudes we should confront them with compassion, and the weapons of arrogance and anger will be broken to pieces. The Buddha said, "Though a single man may defeat a thousand foes, forbearance before victory is much better," and, "Trying to stop violence with violence will never bring it to an end, only patience can stop violence."

Once there was an old woman named Wang who lived in Jiangdu, Jiangsu Province. As a young girl she became a vegetarian and embraced Buddhism with a particular devotion to Avalokitesvara Bodhisattva. At the age of eighteen, she married Liu Wenzao and bore him three boys and one girl. Later on her husband passed away, and she was left to raise her children on her own.

The Mother arranged for her eldest son to marry a daughter of the Huo family. When her son's new wife came to live with them, she became overbearing and began to bully the other members of the family. She was haughty and arrogant, never showing respect to her elders, frequenting humiliating her mother-in-law. But the old woman merely remained mindful of Avalokitesvara's compassion, and brushed such things aside. She spoke to her daughter-in-law with warm and encouraging words and held her in great esteem.

One day a neighbor could not stand it anymore, and said to the elderly Wang, "Why does your daughter-in-law not show you the slightest honor or respect?"

Wang replied, "My daughter-in-law is able and virtuous. She shows not the slightest lack of honor or respect towards me."

The daughter-in-law was secretly listening to what her mother-in-law had to say, and afterwards felt ashamed and regretful. Her sharp, blade-like mind was shattered to pieces by her mother-in-law's patience.

Patience like this arises from the mind of universal compassion. The *Lotus Sutra* mentions a bodhisattva named *Chang Buqing* (常 不輕), "never disparaging." Whenever this bodhisattva would meet someone he would say, "I dare not disparage you, for all will become Buddhas."

No matter how someone rebuked or maligned him, he would still say to that person, "I dare not disparage you." Some would use clubs or stones to beat and strike him, but he would still respond loudly, "I dare not disparage you, for all will become Buddhas." Since he was always saying such words, everyone began to call him "never disparaging."

The phrase "all will become Buddhas" shows respect for the character of other people. One who respects others in this way will not treat them with arrogance or hatred. Later on in the *Lotus Sutra* it is revealed that this bodhisattva is, in fact, Sakyamuni Buddha in a previous life and that he told this story to teach living beings.

The mind of universal compassion is the mind of Avalokitesvara Bodhisattva. With such a mental state, how can anyone attack you? Someone who has a mind of universal compassion is willing to give away everything that belongs to him, even his own life. For a person like this, even the pain of life and death is not worth mentioning.

We should practice the path of universal compassion, for it is eternal and right. We should happily dedicate our lives to pursuing it. To experience the path is great wisdom; from great wisdom comes great compassion; and from great compassion comes great courage.

Great wisdom enables us to clearly understand the principles of reality. When the phenomena of reality is truly understood, then the cycle of birth and death will be seen as waves churning across the great ocean. Though the waves may flow this way and that, the churning of the waves does not increase or decrease the size of the ocean by a single drop. The waves cannot be separated from the water, and the water cannot be separated from the waves. Enlightenment is the same way: *nirvana* does not arise or cease, but is present in this very body within the cycle of birth and death. There is no need to worry about life or death. The Chan School of Buddhism even calls the moment of enlightenment "the experience of dying." In this moment we perceive the oneness of life and death. By entrusting the matter of life and death to Avalokitesvara Bodhisattva, the mind becomes calm and composed. This happens when the mind has no other thoughts or any sense of arrogance.

The Calamity of Evil Spirits

If a great three thousand-fold world system was full of *yaksas* and *raksas* seeking to torment people, and they heard someone call the name of Avalokitesvara Bodhisattva, these evil demons would not even be able to see that person with their evil eyes, much less do any harm.

The fifth calamity is the calamity of evil spirits. A "great three thousand-fold world system" is a unit of cosmological measurement used throughout the Buddhist sutras, roughly equal to a cluster of galaxies. Specifically, a "small world system" encompasses all the celestial bodies and their moons that a sun shines upon (a solar system). One thousand of these world systems is called a "small thousand-fold world system," while one thousand of these systems is called a "medium thousand-fold world system," and one thousand of these systems is called a "large thousand-fold world system." When taken together a small thousand-fold world system, a medium thousand-fold world system, and a large thousand-fold world system are called a "great three thousand-fold world system."

This huge expanse of space is also sometimes called a "Buddha land," because it is said to be the area of influence within which a single Buddha teaches the Dharma. For the sake of scale, the Buddha land of Amitabha Buddha is said to be separated from the Buddha land of Sakyamuni Buddha by one trillion Buddha lands. For all intents and purposes this is limitless, innumerable distance, but the expression "one trillion Buddha lands" gives this abstract concept a concrete expression. In the same way, to say that a great three thousand-fold world system is the area in which a single Buddha teaches the Dharma is just a concrete expression of an abstract concept. There is no need to get bogged down by specific numbers.

The *yaksas* mentioned in the passage are a class of malevolent beings similar to the *raksas* mentioned earlier. Specifically, *yaksas* is Sanskrit for "agile," for such beings are said to be able to fly one million miles in an instant.

Yaksas and *raksas* are simply beings which do harm to the world and to human beings, and in this sense our world is full of *yaksas* and *raksas*. All manner of temptations, including sexual attraction, money, power, fame, status, and many other such temptations too numerous to count are *yaksas* and *raksas*.

The Buddhist sutras commonly give the number of "eighty-four thousand afflictions," though there are many more. Each affliction is like a thief, stealing our virtue, and the *yaksas* and *raksas* are the leaders of these millions of bandits. These *yaksa* bandit-leaders are the three poisons of greed, anger, and ignorance, and their supreme commander is the attachment to self.

Afflictions such as this are a terrible scourge, and if we can get rid of the attachment to self there will be no need to fear anything. However, we cannot seize the supreme commander of this bandit army based solely upon our own strength. Thus our afflictions remain, and we remain confused and unable to focus.

The *Transcendent Sun and Moon Samadhi Sutra* states:

> There are four kinds of demons: demons of the body, demons of sensual desire, demons of death, and demons of heaven. When two pieces of wood are rubbed together, fire can be produced, and the wood burns. Fire does not come from water, wind, or earth. The four demons are like this; they all arise from the mind, not from the outside. It is comparable to the way a painter draws a painting, for the work of his craft is completed through the combination of causes and conditions. Though there be paints, a flat surface, and a brush, if the painter does not paint, then there can be no painting. So too is the multitude of demons, for if one's own mind

is firm and resolute, nothing arises and the four
demons will not appear.

However, the four kinds of demons mentioned in the
Transcendent Sun and Moon Samadhi Sutra cannot arise if the
mind is firm and resolute. The mind can be made firm and resolute when we abide in universal compassion and directly perceive
the true reality of phenomena. With a mind like this, we will no
longer grasp at the illusory self. If we single-mindedly call the
name of Avalokitesvara towards these ends, then no evil spirits
will be able to glare at us. How then will they be able to do us any
harm?

The Calamity of Imprisonment

**If someone, whether guilty or not guilty, who
is bound and fettered with manacles, shackles, and cangue calls the name of Avalokitesvara
Bodhisattva, then all the bonds will be broken, and
that person will instantly attain liberation.**

The sixth calamity is the calamity of imprisonment. In Chinese,
the specific types of binding refer to chains which restrain the
hands, feet, neck, and body. The passage refers to someone whose
freedom and movement are completely restricted.

The benefits of calling the name of Avalokitesvara Bodhisattva
are similar to those discussed with the earlier calamities—one who
is imprisoned may call the name and be freed. But the important
detail to analyze in this passage is the nature of the imprisonment.
Specifically, who is imprisoning you? The manacles, shackles, and

cangue mentioned in the passage refer to the means by which we bind ourselves.

We may have imprisoned ourselves because of a sense of guilt, such that we wish to suffer because of this guilty feeling and not be free. We may have done nothing wrong at all, but we still torment ourselves, blaming everyone and everything. Is the pain that comes from condemning others anything other than a trap of our own making?

We can also be manacled by fame and honor, shackled by fortune, and beset with the cangue of love and attachment to the self. These are the things we use to place ourselves in bondage. We may wish for a good reputation but be unable to achieve it, hope for good fortune and have those hopes dashes, or hem and haw over love and attachment. These are the anxieties of a prisoner. Such people cannot enjoy life, no matter whatever good cause they fight for, how wealthy they may be, how lofty their position, or how fine their reputation.

There is an old Chinese saying: "Do nothing for the sake of fame, or money, or to preserve one's own life. This is the only way to accomplish something great." There are far too few people who can actually let go of such things. The vast majority of people are willing to enslave themselves for money, abandon justice, reason, and human compassion for the sake of fame and honor, becoming mean and cowardly grasping at life. Such people have imprisoned themselves, and can't seem to find a way out, no matter how they try, for they have lost their sense of right and wrong, and lack a sense of justice.

By abiding within the mind of Avalokitesvara Bodhisattva, we break the chains of self-attachment and treat all beings equally. We can then realize that fame and fortune are unreal, for they are merely the combination of causes and conditions, and that birth and death are simply phenomena that are constantly in flux. When illuminated by this wisdom the chains of our bondage will be broken, and we will obtain freedom and comfort.

No one else is able to imprison us; this is something we can only do to ourselves. Even if were to be bound up with physical chains, as long as we maintain a mind like that of Avalokitesvara Bodhisattva, there is no place we cannot feel free.

Before he joined the monastic order, the Tang dynasty Chan master Zhijue served as a local prefect. While he was serving as prefect a famine broke out, and the people in his locality were on the verge of starvation. Unable to bear it any longer, he ordered that the imperial granaries be opened to offer aid to victims of the famine.

But even a government official faces serious criminal charges if he opens the imperial granary on his own without orders from the central government. Zhijue was arrested and put in chains. By imperial edict he was taken under guard to the capital where he was to be put to death.

Zhijue had already realized well in advance that he was sacrificing his life in doing what he did, and he willingly accepted his fate. The emperor was quite familiar with Zhijue's character, and upon hearing of this affair, he knew there must be more to what had happened, so he ordered his men to watch for anything unusual from Zhijue and to report back to him.

On the day of his execution, Zhijue was taken from prison to face his beheading. Even as the blade was raised to cut off his head, his expression did not change. He smiled and said, "I give this life of mine as an offering to all living beings."

Hearing this, the executioner put down his blade and reported what was said to the emperor. Shortly thereafter, an edict was issued ordering a more detailed inquiry. For his part, Zhijue answered with the facts of the matter.

What Zhijue did flowed completely from his great compassion, and he acted without the slightest error or defect. He was willing to sacrifice his own life to save living beings from starvation. Such an act is truly great, but personal considerations could not prevail over the laws of the land. Though his life was spared, he was commanded to join the monastic order, and thus became Chan Master Zhijue.

The Calamity of Brigands

If a great three thousand-fold world system were full of malevolent brigands, and a merchant chief were leading many merchants carrying valuable treasures along a perilous road, and among them one man were to speak up and say, "Good men, do not be afraid. You should call the name of Avalokitesvara Bodhisattva with single-minded effort, for this bodhisattva can bestow fearlessness upon living beings. If you call his name, then you will surely be liberated from these malevolent brigands!" and upon hearing this, if all of the merchants were to call out: "I take refuge in Avalokitesvara Bodhisattva," then by calling his name, they would instantly attain liberation.

The last of the seven calamities is the calamity of brigands. Our mind can contain a great three thousand-fold world system, and that mind is filled with malevolent brigands.

The "perilous road" in the passage represents the five aggregates. In Buddhism the five aggregates are the five components that make up a living entity: form, feeling, perception, mental formations, and consciousness. In other words, the self.

The merchant chief represents the *alaya* consciousness. *Alaya* is a Sanskrit word meaning "storehouse," and is a type of consciousness that stores up all the karmic seeds we generate. All forms of consciousness arise out of the *alaya* consciousness, and the *alaya* consciousness takes the sense objects of the other forms of consciousness as its own.

In Yogacara philosophy, there are eight types of consciousness, of which the *alaya* consciousness is the eighth. The first five consciousnesses correspond with our five sense organs: the eyes, ears, nose, tongue, and body. Each of these sense organs interacts with an external sense object to produce consciousness. For example, the eyes see forms, and produces visual consciousness; the ears hear sound and create auditory consciousness, and so forth.

The sixth consciousness is the mind consciousness, which synthesizes the first five sense consciousnesses. The seventh consciousness, called *manas*, is the form of consciousness that constructs our sense of self by clinging to things as "mine."

The mind contains both the treasures to attain Buddhahood, as well as the brigands which can lead us to fall into confusion. The *alaya* consciousness contains enlightenment as well as ignorance. But as long as someone has experienced Avalokitesvara's mind of universal compassion, that person can strike down the attachment to self with non-self, repudiate desire with compassion, subdue anger with courage, and illuminate ignorance with wisdom. Someone like this can drive away the malevolent brigands of affliction, and safely cross the perilous road. This is how Avalokitesvara can free us from fear, and why the sutras describe him as granting fearlessness.

The Neo-Confucian philosopher Wang Yangming once said, "Suppressing brigands in the mountains is easy; catching the brigands within the mind is difficult." The brigands within the mind wield vast supernatural powers and can transform themselves at will. They can ascend to the heavens or burrow into the earth, so trying to capture them is no easy task. Anyone who attempts to capture the brigands within the mind in the same way that one would capture robbers is a person of greatness.

Someone who resolves to capture robbers as they steal must realize the danger it poses. A robber faced with capture will do anything to resist imprisonment. But as difficult as it is to capture external robbers, the invisible brigands of the mind are even more formidable. However, if we experience the universal compassion of Avalokitesvara Bodhisattva, capturing these brigands is not difficult.

Long ago there was a monk named Venerable Kuya who once encountered some robbers while traveling by foot. Once he saw the robbers, Venerable Kuya began crying from a sense of compassion.

The robbers then mocked him, "What a truly uncultivated monk you are!"

"No," said Kuya, "I am not sad because I am worried about losing money. When I think about people like yourselves who possess such exceptional strength, more so than ordinary people, I think of the many things you could be doing in the world. I don't know what negative karma you have created in the past, but in becoming robbers now you are making your bad karma much worse. I was thinking about the terrible karmic effects you will suffer in the future. This is why I began to cry without realizing it."

Tears continued to stream down Venerable Kuya's face, and his compassion actually touched the robbers. Later on the robbers formally requested that Kuya act as their teacher and they became his disciples.

There is a another somewhat similar story about a Japanese monk named Shichiri Kojun. One day Shichiri was in his hut when a thief broke in brandishing a knife and commanding the monk to hand over his money.

Shichiri took no notice and simply said, "Alright I will," then took out all of his money and gave it to the thief, who tucked the money the monk had given to him into his robe, and then proceeded to quietly leave the house. At that moment Shichiri suddenly called out to him:

"Wait!"

The thief stopped in his tracks.

"You just requested something from me and are leaving without a word of thanks. How can that be right? Originally, I was going to offer this money to the Buddha. Say a word of thanks in front of the Buddha, and everything will be alright."

Perplexed, the thief blurted out a quick "Thank you," and then left.

Not long afterwards, the thief was arrested while committing another robbery, and he confessed to robbing Shichiri as well. The police officer took the thief to Shichiri who, when questioned, said, "Yes, during the night in question a man did enter my house and asked for money, which I gave him. He didn't steal it—I gave it to him willingly. He even said thank you as he left.

The police officer said, "It may be your intention to save this thief, but he has robbed many other places and his crimes are too severe. We can't let him off this time."

Shichiri then took hold of the thief's hand and said, "I am quite poor, and have already given you all the money I have. I even asked you to thank the Buddha. I am sorry that my goodwill fell short, and was unable to move you, and that you went to steal again."

The thief was speechless, and felt very ashamed. During his stay in prison, the thief could not forget what the monk had said, and after he was released, he ran over to see Shichiri to make amends for his misdeeds. From that point on the thief turned over a new leaf and became a good person. This is the transformational power of compassion.

> **Aksayamati, lofty indeed are the awe-inspiring spiritual powers of the great Avalokitesvara Bodhisattva.**

In the concluding passage Sakyamuni Buddha calls Avalokitesvara Bodhisattva "great." The text reads *mohesa* (摩訶薩), which is a transliteration of the Sanskrit *mahasattva*, meaning "great being." The pairing of *mahasattva* with *bodhisattva* is a kind of extended honorific being applied to Avalokitesvara.

III

The Three Poisons

The Poison of Greed

If any living beings are much given to greed, let them keep in mind and revere Avalokitesvara Bodhisattva, and they will be freed from their greed.

The seven calamities are mentioned in the sutra as coming from outside of ourselves, and after they are enumerated the sutra begins to list internal maladies. As a group, they are called the "three poisons," for they poison our bodies and minds. They are greed, anger, and ignorance.

Of the three poisons, the most dangerous is greed. Greed encompasses desire of all forms, though the most intense desire is sensual desire, most specifically sexual desire.

In terms of survival, sexual desire is certainly necessary. Humans and all living beings rely on sexual desire to reproduce and survive as a species. In this sense sexual desire is not something we can deny. Even from a moral perspective, the bond shared between a husband and wife can have all the greatest aspects of human relationships. It is all right to have sexual desire, but excessive sexual desire can be harmful to both the mind and body.

Sexual desire has a great effect upon our social mores, and in this sense improper sexual desire has the potential to do great harm. Buddhism does make a distinction between skillful sexual relationships and unskillful sexual relationships. The most skillful sexual relationship is a healthy marriage, while an unskillful sexual relationship is one that involves excessive, inappropriate, or illicit behavior.

The Buddhist precepts regarding sex are very detailed, and delve into what is an improper time, improper place, improper purpose, and improper amount to engage in sexual behavior. Engaging in skillful sexual behavior is included in Buddhism's "ten wholesome actions": To refrain from killing, to refrain from stealing, and to refrain from sexual misconduct, to refrain from lying, to refrain from harsh speech, to refrain from duplicitous speech, to refrain from flattery, to refrain from greed, to refrain from anger, and to refrain from ignorance.

The *Satya Nirgrantha Sutra* states:

> If one is not satisfied with one's own wife and enjoys fornicating with the wives of other men, then such a person is shameless, and will suffer without ever knowing happiness.

In the essay "On Curbing Desire," Emperor Wen of the Wei dynasty wrote:

> Nothing can equal lust as the chief evil, for it is easy to engage in immoral sexual behavior. A great

and powerful hero can lose his kingdom and his life because of it; a sophisticated and refined scholar can ruin his reputation and name as a result of it. It starts with a momentary slip, but ends up becoming an irredeemable mistake. The fair beauty of a lotus-like face is a flesh covered skeleton; a pretty one in sensuous makeup is a sharp and deadly blade. Even in the company of women as beautiful as jade and flowers, always think of them as your sisters. If nothing has happened, beware lest you take a misstep; if something has already happened, mend your ways before it is too late.

The *Sutra in Forty-two Sections* states:

Think of elderly women as your mother; think of women slightly older than you as your older sisters; think of women younger than you as your younger sisters; and think of young girls as your daughters. Generate the mind of liberation and extinguish all unwholesome thoughts.

A man could have no better intention toward women than as described above; women can practice this as well by considering men to be like fathers, brothers, and sons. In this way one can eliminate sexual desire.

When unskillful thoughts of sexual desire arise, one should keep in mind the compassion, wisdom, and courage of Avalokitesvara Bodhisattva. By viewing all old men as our fathers and all old women as our mothers, or even viewing all living beings as our sons and daughters, we will treat everyone with respect and all thoughts of sexual desire will vanish.

The Poison of Anger

If any are much given to anger, let them keep in mind and revere Avalokitesvara Bodhisattva, and they will be freed from their anger.

The specific Chinese characters used to describe anger in this passage are *chenhui* (瞋恚). *Chen* means a savage, furious expression, and *hui* means a feeling of resentment. The harm caused by anger has already been detailed in the chapter on the seven calamities, but as this passage refers directly to anger, it may be beneficial to provide a wider context for anger as discussed in the Buddhist sutras. For example, the *Sutra of the Teachings Bequeathed by the Buddha* says, "For stealing merit and plundering virtue, nothing surpasses anger." The *Dharmapada* says:

> The ability to control one's own anger is like controlling a careening carriage; those best at reigning in the mind can dispel darkness and receive illumination.

The *One Hundred Parables Sutra* relates an interesting story about anger. Once a large group of people were talking when they began to complain about a certain individual.

"He may have a bit of integrity," one person said, "but he has two great faults: first, he is quick to anger. Second, he acts rashly."

This went on and on, with each person laying some sort of criticism upon this individual. It just so happened that the person about whom the group was complaining was within earshot, and had heard the whole thing. Suddenly he burst into where the group was meeting and shouted, "What are you saying about me?"

The shouting person then grabbed one member of the group, the first person who had began criticizing him, and threw him to the ground. The rest of the group gasped and protested.

"When have I ever been quick to anger? When have I ever acted rashly? I'm not like that at all! That man was making wild accusations, I had no other choice!"

The *One Hundred Parables Sutra* tells another interesting story. Once there was a turtle sitting in the bottom of a dried out pond, trying to find some water to drink. Two large birds were flying overhead and witnessed how thirsty the turtle was and how much he was suffering, so they decided to help.

The birds swooped down and spoke to the turtle, "Turtle, we can carry you to a place where there is plenty to drink. Just hold onto this stick with your mouth, and the two of us will hold onto each end of the stick with our beaks, then we can lift you into the air with our wings and carry you to where the water is. Just be sure to stay completely still while we are carrying you. Don't say a word."

The turtle agreed to the plan and grabbed onto the stick with his mouth. In no time the trio was flying high into the air. As the turtle passed over a village, a young child saw the trio and laughed, "Ha ha! Look at that turtle being carried by two birds!"

The turtle did not like being made fun of, and this made him very angry. He glowered at the child and retorted, "Hey, what do *you* know...."

Just as he opened his mouth, the turtle lost his grip on the stick, fell to the ground, and died. Our anger, like that of the turtle's, comes from our attachment to the self, and our unwillingness to yield to others.

Anger is a negative emotion that arises as an impulse directed at someone else. But that other person need not become angry as well. If we realize that our anger really has nothing to do with the other party, it will disappear on its own.

By keeping Avalokitesvara Bodhisattva in mind, we can perfectly integrate ourselves and others. When self and other are one, anger cannot possibly arise, nor is there any need for patience. By single-mindedly calling the name of Avalokitesvara Bodhisattva and keeping him in mind, anger cannot possibly arise.

In the *Miscellaneous Treasures Sutra,* the Buddha said, "Winning increases the resentment of others, while losing increases one's own sorrow; to not contend who wins and who loses brings the most happiness!"

One who holds the view that he and others are equal does not care about who wins or loses. This is the view of Avalokitesvara Bodhisattva, and how the mind can triumph over anger. When we feel ourselves begin to get angry, we can sincerely recite, "I take refuge in the great, compassionate Avalokitesvara Bodhisattva," and the mind will become compassionate and patient, and anger and resentment will no longer arise.

Once there was a general who was very intolerant of others, even a slight incident would cause him to burst with anger. Even his wife could do nothing about it, and it became a source of great distress for her.

The general also happened to be a committed Buddhist and regularly recited the names of Buddhas and bodhisattvas, though he was doubtful if he had gained anything from the practice, or if it would ever soften his anger.

One morning the general had become infuriated over some small thing his wife had done, so he went before his Buddha shrine in his angered state to recite the sacred names of the Buddhas and bodhisattvas. As he recited, he suddenly realized how shallow and intolerant he had been. He knew that what he had done in the past was wrong, and he began to feel a sense of peace and clarity within him.

This is what is known as Dharma joy: the feeling of universal illumination and softness. Attaining such a state is what allows us to turn away from anger, and is a benefit of revering Avalokitesvara and keeping him in mind.

The Poison of Ignorance

If any are much given to ignorance, let them keep in mind and revere Avalokitesvara Bodhisattva, and they will be freed from their ignorance.

The poison of ignorance enshrouds wisdom and increases the other two poisons. Ignorance is also the root cause for the cycle of birth and death and the source of the eighty-four thousand afflictions of ordinary beings. As a person's ignorance grows, it leads to wrong views. The karmic effect of holding wrong views is rebirth in the animal realm.

There are two kinds of wrong views: wrong views which arise from false knowledge, and wrong views which arise from not understanding the truth. Wrong views stem from a lack of understanding of Buddhist principles, like the principle of impermanence: everything which arises must cease.

People who hold wrong views may deny karma and insist that good causes do not lead to good effects and that bad causes do not lead to bad effects. Such a person may ask, "Are there not honest people who are poor and dishonest people who are wealthy? Are there not people who respect their parents and fall into illness, and people who disrespect their parents who enjoy health? Karma and cause and effect are nonsense!"

Many hold this view, which stems from a failure to understand causality. Honesty and filial piety occupy the sphere of moral causality; wealth and poverty occupy the sphere of economic causality; and sickness and health occupy the sphere of physical causality. As an example, let us consider a person who is very honest and straightforward, but also spends money impulsively. It is only natural that such a person will be poor. In the same way, an unfilial child who takes care of himself will enjoy good health. Such things are easy to understand, and to misunderstand them is to confuse one sphere of causality with another. Additionally, speaking of cause and effect without considering the past, present, and future, and instead making a determination based solely upon the immediate facts is incorrect. This is an example of the ignorance of holding wrong views.

Even if we understand Buddhist principles, if we fail to fully understand their significance and inner workings, then our understanding is merely an illusion. For example, a person may cry when learning that a relative has died, because he thinks that death is a sad thing. Why not think about the deceased being reborn in Amitabha's pure land? If such a person were to think in this way, there would no longer be any need to feel sad.

To think that we can't always think this way because we cannot abandon our attachments to our feelings is wrong thinking.

Once we understand which views are the wrong views, we can move away from them, but wrong thinking can be a much more difficult problem to solve. We may know what is right, but ignorance can take hold and make us consider all manner of "what ifs." This is another kind of attachment. But, by contemplating the wisdom of Avalokitesvara Bodhisattva, our confusion and ignorance can disappear.

> Aksayamati, Avalokitesvara Bodhisattva possesses such awe-inspiring spiritual powers, and many have benefited from them. This is why living beings should constantly keep him in mind.

Sakyamuni Buddha concludes the passage on the three poisons by once again calling Aksayamati Bodhisattva by name and impressing upon him the power of Avalokitesvara Bodhisattva and the benefits that are possible by being mindful of him.

Comparatively, the seven calamities are minor, for the three poisons of the mind are far more insidious. The awesome spiritual powers of Avalokitesvara have the power to transform greed into compassion, anger into courage, and ignorance into wisdom, and then use these qualities to liberate all living beings.

IV

Two Wishes

If any woman wishes for a male child by worshipping and making offerings to Avalokitesvara Bodhisattva, she will then give birth to a son blessed with merit and wisdom. If she wishes for a female child, she will then give birth to a daughter blessed with well-formed and attractive features, one who has planted the roots of virtue over lifetimes and is cherished and respected by all. Aksayamati, such are the powers of Avalokitesvara Bodhisattva!

This passage mentions a different kind of intercession of which Avalokitesvara Bodhisattva is capable: granting the wish for the birth of a child. "Making offerings" as referred to in this passage has a wide range of meanings, though in general there are three different types of offerings:

1. The offering of reverence, such as building majestic halls and temples.

2. The offering of practice, such as reading the sutras or bow-
    ing before the Buddha.
3. The offering of assistance, such as food, drink, and clothing.

The passage also mentions the child being blessed with "merit
and wisdom," though these two simple terms can be quite complex.
The Chinese reads *fude* (福德), "merit," and *zhihui* (智慧), "wisdom." In a Buddhist context, each character represents different
aspects of merit and wisdom and gives a more detailed analysis of
the blessings of merit and wisdom.

*   *Fu* (福) is the tangible aspect of merit, including being
    granted clothing, food, drink, and shelter.
*   *De* (德) is the spiritual aspect of merit, including being
    granted mental virtues which allow one to progress fur-
    ther on the Way.
*   *Zhi* (智) is the essence of wisdom, which includes good
    judgment and the ability to make the right choices.
*   *Hui* (慧) is the functional aspect of wisdom, such as dis-
    cerning between right and wrong.

According to the passage, if a woman wants to give birth to
a boy, she can make a wish before Avalokitesvara and then give
birth to a boy; if she wants to give birth to a girl, she can make
a wish before Avalokitesvara and give birth to a girl. The boy is
described as being blessed with "merit and wisdom," while the girl
is described as being blessed with "well-formed and attractive features." Though the sutra attributes the blessing of merit and wisdom
for boys and the blessing of well-formed and attractive features
for girls, both blessings actually apply to children of either gender.

Categorically, "merit and wisdom" refers to mental qualities, while "well-formed and attractive features" refers to physical qualities. Both are important, and we should strive for both.

Symbolically, masculinity represents wisdom and femininity represents compassion. Thus, in the same way, one who seeks wisdom can worship and make offerings to Avalokitesvara Bodhisattva and gain Avalokitesvara's clear understanding of the true nature of reality. One who seeks compassion should make his mind like that of Avalokitesvara; by persevering in this practice and not deviating from it, one will naturally become more compassionate. By establishing such respect and devotion, we can attain perfect wisdom and universal compassion. If we worship and make offerings by combining our body, speech, and mind, then Avalokitesvara will never leave us.

The great eleventh-century Chan master Fayan regarded this passage as a form of prenatal education. He taught that a woman hoping for children should focus her mind on the great wisdom and great compassion of Avalokitesvara Bodhisattva. Such mindfulness would then eradicate all forms of ignorance and all wrong views, and her child would grow up with the blessings described in the sutra. Therefore, not only does the passage describe the extensive powers of Avalokitesvara Bodhisattva, but it also has practical applications.

The passage describes the children as being those who have "planted the roots of virtue over lifetimes." Those "roots of virtue" are the elements of good karma, which are present from previous lives and reach fruition in the present life. Buddhism views previous lives, the present life, and future lives as being connected through the relationship of cause and effect.

The "roots of virtue" planted in previous lives bear what become positive karmic effects in the present. If an expectant mother can maintain good conduct and a proper state of mind, she is actually caring for the physical and spiritual growth of her child, so that the child will be endowed with the blessings of merit and wisdom and well-formed and attractive features.

As mentioned previously, the term "merit" includes both tangible good fortune and the virtuous qualities of the mind. There are people in this world who enjoy good fortune, but they are short of virtue. Even though such people may have a lot of money they are still disliked by others. There are also people who are virtuous but lack good fortune; although they are honest and upright, their lives are plagued with misfortune.

The phrase "well-formed and attractive features" refers to a beautiful appearance, but we should pay close attention to the expression "well-formed." The Chinese characters for "well-formed" are *duanzheng* (端正). The second character, *zheng*, can mean "well" or "proper" in terms of one's physical appearance, but it may also refer to proper conduct. In this sense, a person with well-formed features also has circumspect behavior. Buddhism does not focus on physical appearance alone, as can be seen in the following passage from the *Yuye Sutra*:

> A woman with well-formed features cannot be called a beautiful woman. A woman may not only have a well-formed appearance, but must have a mind that is pure and graceful to be called a beautiful woman.

A beautiful woman is not merely someone with attractive and charming looks. It is more important that a person is well-formed, modest, and refined in her mental conduct.

If any living being reveres and worships
Avalokitesvara Bodhisattva, their auspicious merit
will not have been in vain.

There are many who worry that their efforts in relying upon
Avalokitesvara Bodhisattva will bring them no merit, but in the
concluding section of the sutra, the Buddha once again assures the
assembly that those who revere Avalokitesvara Bodhisattva will
not have done so in vain. Their efforts will not have been wasted.

When combined with the previous passages on the seven calamities and the three poisons, this section corresponds to the three
types of karma: physical, verbal, and mental. In the passage on
the seven calamities, the Buddha advises the assembly to "call out"
the name of Avalokitesvara, which corresponds to verbal karma.
When discussing the three poisons, the assembly is told to "keep
in mind and revere" Avalokitesvara, corresponding to mental karma. Finally, in this section those who wish for a child are said to
"worship and make offerings" before Avalokitesvara, corresponding to physical karma. By combining all three types of karma in
our practice, we can fully receive the benefits of Avalokitesvara
Bodhisattva.

V

Exhortation to Practice

After describing the many benefits that can be granted by Avalokitesvara Bodhisattva, the Buddha assures Aksayamati Bodhisattva that the benefits that have just been described are real, attainable, and of great value. All living beings should accept and uphold the name of Avalokitesvara Bodhisattva. Such practices are not at all like making offerings to some wooden tablet for good luck or collecting paper talismans for protection and being done with it.

That is not to say that someone who can be set at ease through these folk beliefs has done anything bad. But our ability to accept and uphold Avalokitesvara's virtues of wisdom, compassion, and courage, such that they enter deep within our minds and we do not lose sight of them, is what really matters.

What is the merit of accepting and upholding the name of Avalokitesvara Bodhisattva? Sakyamuni Buddha offers an analogy by posing a question to Aksayamati:

> "Therefore, let all living beings accept and up-
> hold the name of Avalokitesvara Bodhisattva.

> Aksayamati, suppose someone were to accept and
> uphold the names of as many bodhisattvas as there
> are grains of sand along sixty-two hundred million
> Ganges rivers, and spend a lifetime in making of-
> ferings of food, drink, clothing, lodging, and medi-
> cines to them. What do you think? Would the merit
> for such a good man or good woman be great or
> not?"
>
> Aksayamati replied, "Great indeed, World-
> honored One."

The number given above is so large that it is incalculable.
Sixty-two hundred million is already a massive number, and it
is multiplied by the number of grains of sand in the Ganges, the
great river of India. While the number communicates the idea of
an incalculably large number of bodhisattvas being offered to, no
number mentioned in the sutras is arbitrary. The "six" in sixty-two
hundred million refers to the six great elements of earth, water,
fire, air, space, and consciousness. These six can be broken into
two groups, with earth, water, fire, air, and space encompassing
everything physical, while consciousness encompasses everything
mental.

Sakyamuni Buddha then puts the analogy in the proper context for Aksayamati:

> The Buddha said, "Suppose there is another
> person who accepts and upholds the name of
> Avalokitesvara Bodhisattva, and worships and
> makes offerings to him for a single moment; the
> merit gained by these two people will be exactly the

same without any difference. Such merit cannot be exhausted even in hundreds of millions of billions of kalpas. Aksayamati, such are the immeasurable and limitless benefits of the auspicious merit one obtains from accepting and upholding the name of Avalokitesvara Bodhisattva."

The above is truly a key teaching of Mahayana Buddhism: one may worship and make offerings to countless immeasurable bodhisattvas for a lifetime, while another may only worship and make offerings to Avalokitesvara for a moment, yet the merit each gains is the same.

All phenomena are one, and all phenomena are interrelated. There is in fact no duality that separates the one and the many. One contains everything and everything is contained within the one.

The *Flower Adornment Sutra* mentions how examining a speck of dust can reveal the entirety of the dharma realm. Though some may say it is just a speck of dust on the table, if we were to look into its origins, we would see that a speck of dust can only have fallen where it did because of the combined interaction of all phenomena. If this speck of dust was produced from wastepaper, then the paper and the speck of dust are firmly connected. If we look further we see that the paper is related to trees through the manufacturing process, as well as to the machines involved in its manufacturing and all the components to make those machines. Additionally, the speck is related to all of the workers who work in the paper mill, and all of the clothing, food, and housing used to support these workers and all the people involved in the production of these resources. The speck is also related to the land upon which all of these products are made, and even the sun that shines down upon each of these places. If even one of these elements is lacking, the speck of dust cannot exist as it does.

This is how one contains everything and everything is contained within the one. This same relationship as described in the external, physical world also holds true for our internal, spiritual world. When we see things in this way, we can understand why making a single offering to Avalokitesvara Bodhisattva is equivalent in merit to making offerings to as many bodhisattvas as there are grains of sand along sixty-two hundred million Ganges rivers.

In the same way, when we consider things carefully, the length of a lifetime and a moment are not that different either. Many and few, long and short, far and near, and big and small are all comparative terms that are relative to one another. In absolute terms, there is no real distinction between any of these. All merge together and universally become one.

Any time Avalokitesvara Bodhisattva is mentioned, all Buddhas and bodhisattvas are included as well. As many bodhisattvas as there are grains of sand in sixty-two hundred million Ganges rivers can each be considered manifestations of Avalokitesvara Bodhisattva.

As said earlier, we are all Avalokitesvara Bodhisattva, and the above mentioned concept is what makes that possible. There may be an immeasurably limitless number of living beings, but even so, they are all the same as Avalokitesvara. Asking such questions as, How much? or How long? simply do not apply.

The merit derived from making offerings to all bodhisattvas is subsumed by making offerings to Avalokitesvara, while the names of immeasurable bodhisattvas are subsumed under Avalokitesvara Bodhisattva's name. Religious faith should be consistent; the ability to remain focused is what prevents us from being confused. It is this consistent state of mind that allows us to have compassion, wisdom, and courage, so that we can avoid all forms of danger and have all of our hopes fulfilled. When we are distracted by thought, the mind becomes muddled and confused, and we cannot abide peacefully. To ensure that we are on the path, we should maintain a mind that is focused and does not differentiate.

There is an interesting story regarding consistent faith. Once there were two men who kept protective talismans with them wherever they went. One of the men believed in many deities, and thus had a multitude of talismans that he took with him in his handbag. The other man only revered Avalokitesvara Bodhisattva, and kept a single talisman of Avalokitesvara with him in his bag.

One day the two men were walking together down the road, when unexpectedly, another man leapt in front of them brandishing a knife and slashing at them. In the aftermath, one of the men was slightly wounded, while the other was not wounded at all.

When the unharmed man opened his bag, he saw that his talisman of Avalokitesvara Bodhisattva had been nicked by the knife. Surely, he thought, this was a result of his faith in Avalokitesvara, and the talisman had intervened and protected him from the attack. Thus his faith in Avalokitesvara grew even stronger.

The wounded man was quite unhappy and grumbled, "I am just as faithful as he is. I am very devoted and keep several talismans in my bag. Why wasn't I protected?"

The man felt annoyed and upset, until he heard a voice coming from his bag.

"We're sorry!" the voice said, "It's not that we didn't want to help you. We just weren't sure which one of us should protect you. It would be a terrible breach of etiquette if one of us were to protect you without consulting the others. When the knife was coming towards you, we asked the Celestial Emperor to save you, but he deferred to the King of the Heavens. The King of the Heavens deferred to the Goddess of the Sea, and the Goddess of the Sea deferred to Lord of the Stars. It was when all of this discussion was going on that you were cut by the knife. It is only because the other man only has a single talisman of Avalokitesvara Bodhisattva that he could be saved so quickly."

Consistent faith can save us. If someone does not believe in Avalokitesvara Bodhisattva but chooses to put their faith in many deities instead, then this adulterated faith certainly will not be beneficial.

VI

Manifestations

The Second Question

Aksayamati Bodhisattva said to the Buddha, "World-honored One, how did Avalokitesvara Bodhisattva come to this Saha World? How does he teach the Dharma for the sake of living beings? How does he apply the power of skillful means?"

With the previous question concluded, Aksayamati Bodhisattva asks a second question. The question can be broken down into three main points, roughly corresponding to the three types of karma:

- Physical: How has Avalokitesvara come to this Saha World, and in what form does he manifest himself?
- Verbal: How does Avalokitesvara Bodhisattva teach the Dharma for the sake of living beings?
- Mental: How does Avalokitesvara Bodhisattva apply the power of skillful means to liberate living beings?

The term "Saha World" is a Sanskrit expression which roughly means "land of endurance," and refers to this world that we live in. The *Flower of Compassion Sutra* says, "[this world] is called *saha* because this is where all living beings endure the three poisons and all the various afflictions. As they suffer from such corruption, it is called 'land of endurance'." Sakyamuni Buddha thus manifested a physical form in the Saha World to transform it and liberate living beings from affliction.

In Chinese the term "skillful means" is rendered as *fangbian* (方便). *Fang* refers to a method or technique, while *bian* refers to what is fitting, proper, or expedient. In a Buddhist context, this means applying the proper method to liberate living beings. The *Exegesis on the Words and Phrases in the Lotus Sutra* gives three explanations of the meaning of skillful means:

1. "Means" are the teachings while "skillful" refers to their application, in that one employs various methods to instruct living beings in accordance with their wishes.
2. Skillful means is a mode of practice, in that through the application of skillful means one can lead others into Buddhist practice. One may act in accordance with the wishes of others or in accordance with one's own and instruct living beings using various skillful means.
3. "Skillful" refers to the profound, while "means" is something hidden; such that one dares not guess the intention of others, but teaches the Dharma in accordance with one's own understanding for the benefit of others.

Whether skillful means are defined as acting in accordance with one's own wishes, acting according to the wishes of others, or in some combination of the two, one applied skillful means to liberate living beings. This is the power of skillful means.

What then are the skillful means employed by Avalokitesvara Bodhisattva? Sakyamuni Buddha goes on to list thirty-three forms that Avalokitesvara manifests in to liberate living beings. Specifically, Avalokitesvara seeks to liberate living beings from affliction and lead them to *bodhi*.

The Three Noble Manifestations

> The Buddha told Aksayamati Bodhisattva, "Good men, if there are living beings in this land who should be liberated by someone in the form of a Buddha, then Avalokitesvara Bodhisattva will manifest in the form of a Buddha and teach the Dharma to them."

This passage mentions the form of the Buddha, but what exactly is the form of the Buddha? The Buddha is said to have three aspects or "bodies": the Dharmakaya, the Sambhogakaya, and the Nirmanakaya.

The Dharmakaya is the aspect of the Buddha which encompasses the infinitude of space and time, and is a personification of the truth of the universe. The Buddha's Dharmakaya is not limited to a specific place or time.

The Sambhogakaya is the aspect of the Buddha that is capable of experiencing the truth of the universe. The Sambhogakaya is grounded in enlightenment, pervades the ten directions, and is present for all time.

The Nirmanakaya is the aspect of the Buddha that manifests in the world out of compassion for living beings. It is the aspect of the Buddha that manifests according to the spiritual capacities of living beings, and what is being referred to in the above passage. Sakyamuni Buddha is also seen as a manifestation of the Nirmanakaya: he was born, took the monastic life, cultivated spiritual practices, attained enlightenment, and taught the Dharma for the sake of living beings.

Every Buddha is endowed with these three aspects; and in a sense the three are one. One way to understand the three aspects of the Buddha is with the following analogy: The Dharmakaya is like the science of medicine, the Sambhogakaya is like those who research medical science, and the Nirmanakaya is like the doctors and nurses who use medical science to heal and care for the sick.

The passage mentions that Avalokitesvara Bodhisattva is capable of manifesting the form of a Buddha to teach the Dharma, and as such there is nothing wrong with seeing Sakyamuni Buddha as a manifestation of Avalokitesvara. Avalokitesvara is the truth of the universe and an avatar of compassion, just as Sakyamuni Buddha is. In this way, it does not really matter if Sakyamuni Buddha is Avalokitesvara, or if Avalokitesvara is Sakyamuni Buddha.

> **For those who should be liberated by someone in the form of a *pratyekabuddha*, then he will manifest in the form of a *pratyekabuddha* and teach the Dharma to them. For those who should be liberated by someone in the form of a *sravaka*, then he will manifest in the form of a *sravaka* and teach the Dharma to them.**

The next passage mentions Avalokitesvara Bodhisattva's ability to manifest as a *pratyekabuddha* and a *sravaka.* "Pratyekabuddha" is a Sanskrit term that refers to someone who has awakened on their own, without the guidance of a teacher. As such, people who lived before the time of the Buddha or in places where the Buddha's teaching had not yet penetrated and experienced some portion of the truth could be regarded as *pratyekabuddhas.* For example, one could say that the philosophers of Greece and the sages of China are all *pratyekabuddhas.*

This is one of Buddhism's strengths: within the Buddhist teachings there is no narrow-minded notion that only those who receive Sakyamuni Buddha's teachings can attain liberation. As mentioned in the passage, for those who have the potential to be liberated by a *pratyekabuddha,* Avalokitesvara will manifest the form of a *pratyekabuddha* and teach the Dharma to them. Great figures such as Socrates, Plato, Confucius, Jesus, and Mohammed can all be seen as manifestations of Avalokitesvara responding to specific conditions.

Just as there is one moon that hangs in the sky which can be reflected in rivers, waterways, seas, or oceans, so too is there one universal truth that can be experienced in many ways. This is how the many manifestations of Avalokitesvara Bodhisattva can teach and liberate living beings by adapting to different epochs and regions.

Pratyekabuddhas are said to attain enlightenment not from receiving the teachings of the Buddha, but by observing the Dharma within the world, specifically in coming to realize the truth of dependent origination. Each of who are traveling through the cycle of birth and death take part in dependent origination, but our wisdom is obscured by our ignorance and we do not come to understand how dependent origination works.

There are twelve links in the cycle of dependent origination:

1. **Ignorance** leads one to developing mental formations.
2. **Mental formations** generate consciousness.
3. **Consciousness** causes one to start making distinctions, which leads to name and form.
4. **Name and form** interact with the external world and generate the six sense organs.
5. **The six sense organs**, the eye, ear, nose, tongue, body, and mind, encounter external sense objects, creating contact.
6. **Contact** between the sense organs and sense objects generates feeling.
7. **Feeling** naturally leads to craving
8. **Craving**, when it is fixated upon, becomes grasping.
9. **Clinging** causes one to try to hold onto one's cravings, and further becoming.
10. **Becoming** leads one again to experience birth.
11. **Birth** leads to the suffering of aging and death.
12. **Aging and death**, unless one cultivates the Dharma, leads to future rebirth and continued ignorance.

The cycle thus keeps on continuing. In short, our delusion leads us to generate negative karma, and when this negative karma reaches fruition we suffer. Suffering leads to more delusion, and the cycle continues.

The passage also mentions Avalokitesvara's ability to manifest in the form of a *sravaka*. *Sravaka* is a Sanskrit term that means "voice-hearer," and refers to a disciple of the Buddha who listens to the Buddha's teaching on the Four Noble Truths:

1. There is a mass of suffering in this world.
2. Suffering is caused by the accumulation of negative physical, verbal, and mental karma.
3. Suffering can end by ending this accumulation.
4. To end this accumulation and attain enlightenment one must practice the Noble Eightfold Path.

The basic teachings of Buddhism are encapsulated in the Four Noble Truths: ignorance causes suffering, and ignorance is an effect of negative karma. Enlightenment causes suffering to end, and enlightenment is an effect of the practicing the Noble Eightfold Path. All beings who listen to the Four Noble Truths and attain enlightenment are *sravakas*.

All the sutras, from Early Buddhism to Mahayana Buddhism, were developed from the Four Noble Truths. While *sravaka* means "voice-hearer," this does not mean that only people born during the time of the Buddha and heard his voice are *sravakas*, for the Buddha's teachings are still found in the world today. The Buddhist canon as we know it today is built on the recollections of the Venerable Ananda who was the Buddha's attendant and personally heard the Buddha's discourses. These recollections have since been written down, translated, and spread to all parts of the world, and function as the "voice" of the Buddha teaching the Dharma.

A *sravaka* can be any disciple of the Buddha who joined the monastic order, followed the Buddha's teachings, cultivated their practice, and attained enlightenment. Avalokitesvara Bodhisattva can manifest as whatever type of disciple will bring liberation to living beings. In this sense, the great monastics of history can be considered manifestations of Avalokitesvara Bodhisattva, including

Asvaghosa, Nagarjuna, Bodhidharma, Zhizhe of the Tiantai School, Fazang Xianshou of the Huayan School, Huiyuan and Shandao of the Pure Land School, Dengyo Daishi, Kobo Daishi, and Nichiren. All of these great monastics are examples of *sravakas* who taught the Dharma out of compassion for living beings.

In some Buddhist sutras *sravakas* are described as oppositional to Mahayana Buddhism, so some may wonder if it is correct to describe some of these great Mahayana monastics as *sravakas*. However, there are two kinds of *sravakas*. Those who reject Mahayana teachings are called "*sravakas* who are deluded regarding the Dharma," while those who embrace Mahayana teachings are called "*sravakas* of extensive wisdom." Additionally, Avalokitesvara will manifest in whatever form is necessary to liberate others, and if living beings can be liberated by a *sravaka* who rejects Mahayana teachings, then he will manifest in that form.

Manifestation as Celestial Kings

For those who should be liberated by someone in the form of King Brahma, then he will manifest in the form of King Brahma and teach the Dharma to them. For those who should be liberated by someone in the form of Lord Sakra, then he will manifest in the form of Lord Sakra and teach the Dharma to them. For those who should be liberated by someone in the form of Isvara, then he will manifest in the form of Isvara and teach the Dharma to them.

This passage lists Avalokitesvara's manifestations as the various gods of India. In order to understand the purpose of Avalokitesvara's manifestations as these gods, there are a number of lines of inquiry that must be followed.

First we should understand exactly who the gods being mentioned are. For example, King Brahma and Lord Sakra (also called Indra) have been part of India's religions since ancient times. From a Buddhist perspective, all the deities of the Brahmans have lead many people to adopt a proper way of living and enter the path to enlightenment. For this reason Buddhism does not reject these deities in any way. Additionally, there are many people who turn to Buddhism having first started worshipping these deities, so they should not be discounted. The gods mentioned above are honored because they are still superior to ordinary people, even though their spiritual practices cannot directly lead one to Buddhahood.

The Buddhist conception of the universe is based on the tradition of India, and has a similar cosmology. According to Buddhist cosmology, the universe can be divided into three realms: the desire realm, the form realm, and the formless realm. The goal of Buddhist practice is to transcend these three realms, for the *Lotus Sutra* says, "The turmoil of the three realms is like a burning house."

The desire realm is comprised of the six realms discusses earlier: hell, the realm of hungry ghosts, the animal realm, the *asura* realm, the human realm, and heaven. The "Heaven" realm actually includes many other heavenly realms, inhabited by various classes of celestial beings.

According to Indian tradition, at the center of each world system is an inconceivably large mount called Mount Sumeru. There are four continents surrounding Mount Sumeru, one in each of the cardinal directions. The eastern continent is called Videha, the western continent is called Godaniya, the northern continent is called Kuru, and the southern continent is called Jambu, which is where we live.

Halfway up Mount Sumeru dwell the four heavenly kings: Dhrtarastra in the east, Virupaksa in the west, Virudhaka in the south, and Vaisravana in the north. At the top of Mount Sumeru is the Trayastrimsat Heaven, "heaven of thirty-three gods," is said to be inhabited by eight gods in each of the cardinal directions with Lord Sakra at its center.

Beyond Mount Sumeru there is a group of heavenly realms called the "sky heavens," which include Tusita Heaven, Nirmanarati Heaven, and Paranirmita-vasavartin Heaven. This is the extent of the heavens in the desire realm. Beings who inhabit the heavens beyond the desire realm no longer have any desires. The form realm contains heavens corresponding to the four *dhyanas*, which are ever increasing levels of meditative absorbtion. King Brahma is said to reside in the heaven of the first *dhyana*.

Beyond the heavens of the form realm lie the heavens of the formless realm. Beings who reside in these heavens not only are free from all desire but they have no physical bodies. The heavens of the formless realm correspond to the four formless *dhyanas*, which are even higher levels of meditative attainment. These are the heaven of infinite space, the heaven of infinite consciousness, the heaven of nothingness, and the heaven of neither thought nor non-thought. These many heaven realms can be seen as a representation of spiritual progress, of ascending meditative absorption and quiescence.

That being said, when Avalokitesvara chooses to manifest as a deity, not only does he manifest the physical form of that deity, but also the mind of the deity as well. When Avalokitesvara manifests as King Brahma he also manifests the mind of King Brahma, and when he manifests as Lord Sakra he also manifests the mind of Lord Sakra.

Typically, a bodhisattva manifests in a form that is similar to the person he is trying to help, so that he can skillfully assimilate. Bodhisattvas use their empathy to work alongside those whom they are trying to liberate so they can better guide them. This is like a mother trying to get her child to eat; she will, often without thinking about it, open her mouth as well.

Looking at it from another perspective, Avalokitesvara Bodhisattva manifests as King Brahma or Lord Sakra in order to transform our own minds to be like the minds of King Brahma and Lord Sakra. We should look within our own minds and manifest the great compassion of Avalokitesvara Bodhisattva. If we are committed to self-cultivation, this is something we should really think about.

The *Treatise on the Abhidharma* describes heaven as "an illumination of light." Regardless of the context, whenever Buddhism speaks of light it is always a metaphor for wisdom. The light of wisdom is obscured by the darkness of human desire. Though beings who reside in the realm of the four heavenly kings still have desire, it is only a scant amount. Those beings who reside in Lord Sakra's heaven no longer have any sensual desire, though some subtle forms of mental desire still abide. In the Brahma heaven, the first heaven of the form realm, all desire is gone and the beings who reside there constantly enjoy a state of quiescent purity. The heaven realm immediately beyond the Brahma heaven is called the Mahabrahma heaven, of which the *Suramgama Sutra* says:

> [One who is] perfected in mind and body, not lack-
> ing in dignified demeanor, observes the precepts

in purity, and has attained clear understanding
can unite the followers of Brahma to become the
great King Brahma. A grouping of such individuals is called the Mahabrahma heaven.

The deity "Isvara" mentioned in the passage is actually a wicked
deity. The heaven of Isvara is filled with evil deities who interfere
in the human world and do all they can to harm the Dharma. The
realm of Isvara is called the Paranirmita-vasavartin heaven, and
is the sixth and highest heaven of the desire realm. Paranirmita-
vasavartin means "partaking in the pleasures created by others" in
Sanskrit. The *Treatise on the Perfection of Great Wisdom* defines
this heaven by saying, "Beings of this heaven seize whatever is
created by others for their own enjoyment, hence the name 'paranirmita-vasavartin.'" The first chapter of the *Commentary on the
Verses from the Abhidharma* also says, "The beings of Paranirmita-
vasavartin heaven obtain their pleasure from what others have
created."

Why would Avalokitesvara manifest as an evil deity? While
Avalokitesvara manifests as a good deity to inspire those who are
good, he is also capable of manifesting as an evil deity as a warn-
ing to those who are wicked. Avalokitesvara uses both acceptance
and subjugation as skillful means to liberate living beings. Love
without force is not often complied with, while force without love
invites resistance.

The spiritual capacity of living beings varies greatly, and
Avalokitesvara's manifestations also vary according to the given
conditions. Some are led to do good when they hear of the good
deeds of others, while seeing the wrongdoing of others can help
some to examine their own wrongdoing.

If we are pure, this is Avalokitesvara manifesting as King Brahma within our minds. If we practice the ten wholesome actions of refraining from killing, stealing, sexual misconduct, lying, duplicitous speech, harsh speech, flattery, greed, anger, and ignorance, then this is Avalokitesvara manifesting as Lord Sakra within our minds to guide us. If we have unwholesome thoughts, this is Avalokitesvara manifesting as Isvara within our minds to encourage us to reflect on ourselves and realize our faults.

> **For those who should be liberated by someone in the form of the Mahesvara, then he will manifest in the form of the Mahesvara and teach the Dharma to them. For those who should be liberated by someone in the form of a great heavenly general, then he will manifest in the form of a great heavenly general and teach the Dharma to them. For those who should be liberated by someone in the form of Vaisravana, then he will manifest in the form of Vaisravana and teach the Dharma to them.**

The first deity mentioned in this passage, Mahesvara, is realted to Isvara of the previous passage. Mahesvara is an evil deity that rules the highest heaven of the form realm. Mahesvara's heaven is called Akanistha, "the extreme border of the form realm." Mahesvara is depicted as a being with three eyes and eight arms who rides a white bull.

The *Vimalakirti Sutra* gives a good explanation to why Avalokitesvara manifests as evil deities:

> Thereupon Vimalakirti then asserted to Mahakasypa: "Now sir, those who appear as demon kings in the countless and immeasurable worlds of the ten directions are mainly liberated bodhisattvas. They [employ their powers of skillful means in order to] guide and transform living beings, which is why they manifest in the form of demon kings."

The great heavenly general mentioned in the passage is the general of Lord Sakra's army, who is sometimes called Narayana, "unshakeable warrior." When Lord Sakra fought with the *asuras*, his forces were led by this general. At the main gate of Buddhist temples there are statues of the two kings: the one on the left is the unshakable warrior Narayana, and the one on the right is the adamantine warrior Guhyapada, both of whom are called heavenly generals. This manifestation specifically draws attention to Avalokitesvara's great courage, as he manifests as a great heavenly general to protect the Dharma.

The manifestation of Vaisravana is known to brahmans as the guardian of wealth. He is said to live within the nine crystal palaces on the fourth level of Mount Sumeru and is the ruler of the *yaksas* and *raksas* in the north. He is said to have taken refuge in the Buddha and is worshipped by the Tiantai School and Mantra School of Buddhism. The *Sutra of the Heavenly King Vaisravana* describes him as having ten blessings:

1. The blessing of contentedness.
2. The blessing of long life.

3. The blessing of family, which is the karmic effect of generosity.

4. The blessing of understanding, which is the karmic effect of morality.

5. The blessing of love and respect, which is the karmic effect of patience.

6. The blessing of a conquering army.

7. The blessing of fields of bountiful harvest.

8. The blessing of ample food, which is the karmic effect of diligence.

9. The blessing of Buddhahood, which is the karmic effect of meditative concentration.

10. The blessing of wisdom, which shines forth from meditative concentration.

It is important to note that the blessings of Vaisravana are products of the positive karma generated from his practice of the six perfections. Each of us who cultivates the six perfections can attain these blessings as well.

The first of the ten blessings, the blessing of contentedness, is the most important. It is also called the inexhaustible blessing, for one's contentedness can never be exhausted.

The wondrous voice of Avalokitesvara enters the heavenly realms to teach the Dharma with great compassion and thus liberate living beings. However, it is important to remember that whether Avalokitesvara manifests as King Brahma, Lord Sakra, Isvara, Mahesvara, the great heavenly general, or Vaisravana, these heavenly realms are not distant, for they exist within each of our minds.

Manifestation as Human Leaders

> For those who should be liberated by someone in
> the form of a lesser king, then he will manifest in
> the form of a lesser king and teach the Dharma to
> them. For those who should be liberated by some-
> one in the form of an elder, then he will manifest in
> the form of an elder and teach the Dharma to them.
> For those who should be liberated by someone in
> the form of a layperson, then he will manifest in the
> form of a layperson and teach the Dharma to them.
> For those who should be liberated by someone in
> the form of a minister, then he will manifest in the
> form of a minister and teach the Dharma to them.
> For those who should be liberated by someone in
> the form of a brahman, then he will manifest in the
> form of a brahman and teach the Dharma to them.

This passage describes Avalokitesvara Bodhisattva's manifestation
as various human beings in positions of power or authority, including lesser kings, elders, laypeople, ministers, and brahmans.

The kings mentioned in the passage are referred to as "lesser"
kings to distinguish them from the manifestations mentioned in
the previous passage, who are the celestial kings. The term "lesser
king" refers to all kings and political leaders in the human realm or
greater or lesser standing in any country.

In other texts human kings are sometimes referred to in
Chinese as *susan wang* (粟散王), "scattered millet kings." This is
because the human world there are many kings scattered across
the world in various countries, like grains of millet cast across the

earth. While each king may feel he is grandiose, from the perspective of the universe, he is quite small and scattered.

In the *Suramgama Sutra* the Buddha says of his own powers of manifestation:

> Now all living beings would enjoy being human kings, and so I manifest in the form of a human king before them in order to teach the Dharma, enabling them to attain [the Way].

Kings and rulers have the ability to liberate their people through the example of their courage and wisdom. In this sense we can see the wise and sagely rulers of the past as manifestations of Avalokitesvara Bodhisattva, such as King Ashoka of India, Emperor Wen of the Sui dynasty, Emperor Taizong of the Tang dynasty, Emperor Hongwu of the Ming dynasty, Emperor Shunzhi of the Qing dynasty, Prince Zhaoming of the Liang dynasty, and Prince Shotoku of Japan. Each of these rulers were great patrons of Buddhism and did all they could to spread its teachings.

The *Sutra on the Contemplation of the Mind* lists ten responsibilities of a virtuous ruler. Without fulfilling these ten responsibilites, a king cannot rightly be called a manifestation of Avalokitesvara. They are as follows:

1. He should look upon the world with the wisdom eye.
2. He should adorn the country with great merit and wisdom.
3. He should confer peace and joy upon the people.
4. He should subdue all hostile enemies.
5. He should remove disasters and dispel terror.

6. He should gather all wise and virtuous men to take charge of state affairs.

7. He should guarantee the people security within the country's borders.

8. He should manage the affairs of state in accordance with the law.

9. He should shoulder the responsibility for the karma of the country.

10. He should have such leadership that all subjects see him as their master.

The next manifestation in this group is the form of an elder. The term in Chinese is *zhangzhe* (長者), which literally refers to an older person, but is commonly used in Chinese to refer to someone who is wealthy and established. However, to truly be considered an "elder," wealth is not enough. According to the *Glossary of Translated Terms*, an elder must possess ten qualities—five material, and five mental.

Material Qualities	Mental Qualities
Respectable Lineage	Wisdom
High Rank	Pure Conduct
Great Wealth	Propriety
Impeccable Manners	Renown
Seniority	Leadership

In Chinese, "layperson" is rendered as *jushi* (居士), and the term is commonly used to refer to the Buddhist laity. The *Annotated Sayings of the Patriarchs* says that a layperson should possess four qualities:

1. He should refrain from seeking official office.
2. He should be virtuous and have few desires.
3. He should have great wealth in money and property.
4. He should find joy in acting in accordance with the Way.

The *Ten Part Vinaya* says:

> Besides kings, royal ministers, and brahmans, lay-men are those who live at home as commoners dressed in white. These are called lay Buddhist practitioners.

The *Suramgama Sutra* states:

> If there are living beings who love to discuss wise sayings and live pure and quiet lives, then I will manifest in the form of a layperson before them and teach the Dharma, enabling them to attain the Way.

The next manifestation, "minister," in Chinese rendered as *zaiguan* (宰官), refers to any official who assists with governance or is involved in political matters. In the *Suramgama Sutra* the Buddha describes his own manifestations in this way:

> If there are living beings who love to rule territo-ries and divide up city-states, then I will manifest in the form of a minister before them and teach the Dharma, enabling them to attain the Way.

In ancient China there was an extensive system of civil service involving nine levels of government officials who helped to govern in accordance with the law. Any such person, from the great advisors in the court of the emperor to a village chief can be considered a minister. If all the ministers in a country would conduct themselves as if they were manifestations of Avalokitesvara Bodhisattva, then the country would be in good order.

The manifestation of the brahman refers to the caste system of ancient India, in which brahman was the highest caste. The caste system, beginning with those of the highest station in society to the lowest is as follows:

1. The brahman caste, comprised of priests and religious people.
2. The kshatria caste, comprised of rulers and warriors.
3. The vaisia caste, comprised of merchants and tradespeople.
4. The sudra caste, comprised of farmers and laborers.

"Brahman" refers to those people who are pure in their practice, have a lofty character, and have given up unwholesome beliefs. They are learned and well-informed, belonging to this highest class of priests and scholars within the four castes. Brahmans claim that, at the beginning of time, the great creator-god Brahma was split into several pieces, and that the Brahman caste was born from Brahma's mouth. They are the most exalted caste, and their authority exceeds that of the Kshatria, for they believe that they transmit the holy messages of the gods. Upon birth, members of this group are expected to strictly observe religious discipline, and upon reaching manhood, they must master their religious texts, called the four Vedas and the eighteen classics. At age forty, fearing that their family line will die out, they return home to marry and produce a son and heir. At fifty, they return to spiritual practice and become mendicants.

The distinctions between the four castes led to great inequalities. Castes were generally not allowed to intermarry, nor could the lower castes enjoy the same rights and benefits as the brahmans or kshatria. The division between rich and poor in ancient India was quite astounding.

Buddhism completely opposed the inequalities of the caste system. Throughout India, anyone joining the monastic order, regardless of their caste background, was regarded as part of the Buddha's family without exception.

In the context of the sutra, the manifestation of the brahman refers to that of a priest or religious person of any denomination. For those who can be liberated by them, Avalokitesvara will also manifest as a Confucian scholar, a clergyman, or a missionary of another religion. This attitude towards non-Buddhists is one of the greatest qualities of Buddhism.

Manifestation as Buddhist Practitioners

For those who should be liberated by someone in the form of a *bhiksu*, a *bhiksuni*, an *upasaka*, or an *upasika*, then he will manifest in the form of a *bhiksu*, a *bhiksuni*, an *upasaka*, or an *upasika* and teach the Dharma to them.

The next group of manifestations is made up of the four groups of Buddhist followers. *Bhiksu* refers to a male mendicant, and *bhiksuni* refers to a female mendicant. They are called mendicants because they beg for the Dharma from the Buddhas to support their wisdom and they beg for food from people to sustain their bodies. Worldly beggars only beg for food and clothing, not for the Dharma, so they cannot be called *bhiksus*.

There are six common epithets applied to *bhiksus* and *bhiksunis* throughout the Buddhist sutras. They are:

1. Menacer of demons: *Bhiksus* strike fear into demons due to their aspiration to seek enlightenment.
2. Destroyer of thieves: "Thieves" refer to those afflictions which steal our merit and virtue. By practicing the path to enlightenment *bhiksus* destroy all affliction.
3. Mendicant: As stated before, *bhiksus* are also called "mendicants" because they beg for the Dharma from the Buddhas, and beg for food from living beings.
4. Worthy of support: Those *bhiksus* who seek supreme enlightenment are worthy of the offerings of food, clothing, shelter, and medicine.
5. Eliminator of unwholesomeness: By adhering to the monastic rules, *bhiksus* are able to eliminate unwholesome thoughts in the mind.
6. Unborn: *Bhiksus* who have attained enlightenment will not be born into the cycle of birth and death ever again.

Upasaka and *upasika* are Sanskrit terms for male and female lay Buddhist disciples, respectively. An *upasaka* is someone who has received the five precepts and practices the Buddhist teachings. In Sanskrit, the term means "good man nearby," "near dwelling man," or "near serving man," meaning someone who draws near to and serves the Buddha, Dharma, and Sangha. The *Commentary on the Flower Adornment Sutra* explains that *upasakas* are so named because they are close to the *bhiksus* and are entrusted with duties.

In whatever form these lay and monastic disciples of the Buddha can help living beings to be liberated, Avalokitesvara Bodhisattva will manifest in such a form and teach the Dharma.

During the sixth century, at the time of the reign of Emperor Wu of the Liang dynasty, the Chan Patriarch Bodhidharma arrived from India to introduce the Chan teachings to China. When Bodhidharma arrived, Emperor Wu met with him and asked, "What is the ultimate truth of the noble teachings?"

Bodhidharma replied, "This vast expanse has nothing noble."

"Who stands before me?" the emperor asked.

Bodhidharma replied, "I do not know."

Because of their failure to communicate, Bodhidharma left and went to Shoalin Temple on Mount Song. Later, Emperor Wu took refuge with Baozhi, and eventually their conversation turned to the incident of Bodhidharma's arrival. Baozhi said, "Bodhidharma is a manifestation of Avalokitesvara Bodhisattva; he imparts the mind-seal of the Buddha."

This is an example of Avalokitesvara appearing as a *bhiksu* in order to teach the Dharma. Who knows how many stories there are just like this one? Avalokitesvara can indeed manifest as a *bhiksu, bhiksuni, upasaka,* or *upasika* to teach the Dharma to living beings.

Manifestation as Women

For those who should be liberated by someone in the form of a woman who is an elder, a layperson, a minister, or a brahman, then he will manifest in the form of a woman and teach the Dharma to them.

There are some people who think that Buddhism justifies disrespect towards women, but such an attitude is extremely mistaken. There are passages in the Buddhist sutras which advise men who are serious practitioners not to approach women, but this advice is given out of concern that lust may impede their practice. It is not meant to belittle women even the tiniest bit.

Women too can become Buddhas and bodhisattvas. One example of a great Buddhist woman is Queen Srimala. Her teachings given in the *Lion's Roar of Queen Srimala Sutra* were all affirmed by the Buddha. Queen Srimala was regarded as a manifestation of Dipamkara Buddha, but she may as well be seen as a manifestation of Avalokitesvara Bodhisattva.

The passage mentions manifesting as an elder, a layperson, a minister, or a brahman, though there is no need to focus on these terms a second time. All women who possess the virtues of great compassion, great wisdom, and great courage can be seen as manifestations of Avalokitesvara Bodhisattva teaching the Dharma.

Among the three virtues of compassion, wisdom, and courage, the most important is compassion. Avalokitesvara Bodhisattva is commonly depicted manifested in a feminine form because women are often the best representation of compassion. Compassion is one of the best and most ennobling aspects of femininity.

However, in today's society our conception of womanhood often lacks this moral dimension of compassion. Purity and elegance are neglected, and anything can be disregarded for the sake of money. In Asia many people think disregarding their own traditional values for personal gain is being "more western," but to imitate the most superficial external qualities of consumerism in Western culture is dangerous.

As we move forward into the modern age of communication and multiculturalism, we should not forget the fine virtue of modesty. This does not only pertain to women, for men need it too. It is also important not to confuse modesty with timidity. When modesty is mistaken for timidity it can easily become cowardice, and there is nothing good about that.

Manifestation as Children

For those who should be liberated by someone in the form of a young boy or young girl, then he will manifest in the form of a young boy or young girl and teach the Dharma to them.

This passage describes Avalokitesvara's ability to manifest as children. In Chinese, the terms are rendered *tongnan* (童男) and *tongnu* (童女), which generally refer to people who are unmarried. *Tongnan* and *tongnu* can thus be applied to people aged forty or fifty. Considering the context of the sutra, it is better to consider these terms to apply specifically to children. There are many instances when children have done a great deal to teach the Dharma to others.

Long ago in Hiroshima, Japan there lived a man named Kobei,

but the people who knew him called him "Buddha Kobei." He was a poor carriage driver, but he was respected by others because of his great compassion. But Kobei was not always like this. In fact, he used to be wicked and cruel. People were as terrified of him as a poisonous snake, and those who knew him then called him "Devil Kobei." How could his reputation change so drastically?

It began when he had fallen sick and was confined to his bed for a long time, out of work. One night Kobei's wife was rubbing her sick husband's back and told him, "We have sold everything we can. We have no money left at all. I can think of nothing else but to go out begging tomorrow."

Kobei began to cry, and the two were soon weeping together. Their eight-year old son, Manzou, who had been asleep beside them, began to sob beneath his blanket.

"Why are you crying, son?" his mother asked, "Did you have a bad dream?"

"No. Mama, let me go to work as a carriage driver tomorrow. I don't want to have to beg for food!"

Manzou's mother comforted him until he returned to sleep, not knowing that her son was serious. Early the next morning, Manzou led the horse out and was preparing to leave, when his mother saw him. He was too short to put the saddle on the horse's back, but his mother was so moved by her son's determination that she helped him secure the saddle. Little Manzou was soon on his way while his mother stayed home to tend to his sick father, all the while feeling anxious.

That evening, Manzou returned with a small amount of money. He continued to go to work each day, bringing home a little money for his parents.

Many days later, after Devil Kobei had recovered, he went to where the carriage drivers would gather looking for work, and saw his horse tied up with Manzou crying beside it.

"Hey, why are you crying? Is it because your stomach aches? Go out there and find some work!"

"No, I'm not crying because my stomach aches," Manzou said drying his tears. "I'm crying because they didn't give me anything to load today."

"That's why you're crying? It happens all that time. There's nothing you can do about it. Have you eaten yet?"

"No, I haven't had my lunch yet. Since there is no work to do, I bring my lunch home for you and mom."

Kobei was silent, "You mean you don't eat when you don't work?"

"No, I don't," Manzou replied earnestly. Kobei was extremely moved.

"You are part of this family, and you need to eat whatever small amount of food we have," and with that Kobei took his son home. When Manzou's mother heard what had happened she was very upset, and cooked a fish dinner to comfort her son. Manzou ate his rice, but did not touch the fish.

"Why aren't you eating your fish?" his mother asked him.

"I don't feel like eating it. I don't know why." Manzou continued, "I remember that, at home, when both of you were praying, you didn't eat any fish." Manzou had observed his parents observing a vegetarian fast. "That's why I'm not eating any fish."

Kobei was so moved that he began to cry. From that moment forward, he changed his cruel ways and violent temperament. That is how he came to be called Buddha Kobei.

Even though he was just a boy, Manzou can truly be seen as a manifestation of Avalokitesvara Bodhisattva, for he was able to transform Koebi's devilish mind into the mind of a Buddha. Goodness and wickedness are only separated by a barrier as thin as a sheet of paper.

At the end of the first Sino-Japanese war, both countries sent representatives to discuss peace terms at the city of Shimonoseki. China sent as its representative Li Hongzhang, and Japan sent Ito Hirobumi and Mutsu Munemitsu, who was considered Japan's top diplomat at the time. While the peace terms were being discussed, Mutsu's seventeen-year old daughter was bedridden with a serious illness. All her doctors were convinced that her illness was terminal.

Mutsu Munemitsu was a great civil servant charged with the enormous task of peace negotiations. He could not ignore the weighty affairs of the state for personal reasons, and thus Mutsu could not stay with his daughter. As he was about to leave to enter peace negotiations, Mutsu said a few comforting words to his daughter, and gave his family the following grave instruction, that owing to the importance of his task he should not be informed of his daughter's condition, even if it worsened.

The peace negotiations slowly proceeded. As they neared the signing stage, all of the color drained from Mutsu's face. When Ito Hirobumi saw him like this, he asked him what was the matter.

"Nothing! It's nothing!"

Mutsu would not say what was on his mind, and this worried Ito. Ito asked once more, and Mutsu replied in a straightforward manner. "My daughter is terminally ill. I understand that we are about to conclude our negotiations, but I just received a letter from home. My daughter's condition is critical and she said that, before she dies, she needs to ask me something. My own dear daughter knows that her illness is incurable, and she asks to speak to me now. But how can I possibly go back when I am charged with this important task? Thinking about this has made me quite upset. That is why I look as I do."

Ito was sympathetic, and replied, "The documents are ready to sign; you can leave them to me. Hurry home and see your precious daughter."

Hearing this, Mutsu immediately set out for his home. When he finally saw his daughter, she asked, "Daddy, I already know that nothing can save me, and that soon I will die. But where will I go after I die?"

Mutsu Munemitsu was a great national politician, yet he had no idea how to answer this question. Standing before his daughter, he wondered how he had never considered it before. He wanted so much for her to live, but there was nothing he could do. He was her father, but he did not know how to answer her question.

It was a terrible situation. He had discovered a question he had never considered before, and he could not possibly respond in some careless fashion. Mutsu thought about it for a moment, and finally answered.

"Your mother had always entrusted any matter, even life and death, to Avalokitesvara Bodhisattva. I do not know where you will go, but surely you will be guided by Avalokitesvara."

Mutsu's young daughter seemed reassured, and joined her palms in reverence to Avalokitesvara. Then she closed her eyes, and passed from this world.

The incident moved Mutsu to become a Buddhist, and in time he became a great practitioner. To him, his daughter was a manifestation of Avalokitesvara, who had come to open up his confused mind. Mutsu believed this very deeply, and told his story to others.

There is another, similar story about a miserly married couple. They possessed a great deal of wealth and property, but when it came to community matters nearby them, they were so stingy that they would not offer a penny's worth of help. Whenever there was any kind of social gathering where spending money might come up, they were nowhere to be found, but if there was any money to be made, they were in a mad rush to be there first.

The couple had one daughter who was the apple of their eye. Even though they were greedy and miserly in every other way, they doted on their daughter to an extraordinary degree. She got whatever she wanted, and her parents did whatever they could to fulfill her wishes. They did not want her to experience any form of suffering, so they pampered their daughter as much as possible.

However, the things of this world mostly do not go according to our wishes, and eventually their daughter became sick and bedridden. The parents spared no expense on doctors and medicine and did whatever could be done to help her, but nothing worked. She became sicker and sicker, and it became clear that she was approaching the last days of her life. By that time their daughter also knew that she soon would draw her last breath.

The greedy father asked his daughter, "Do you want anything? Just tell us, no matter what it is, mommy and daddy will buy it for you."

The young girl placed her emaciated hand on her father's knee and said, "As I've grown up you've done nothing that went against my wishes, and in that sense I am quite content. But I still have one wish. If it is fulfilled, I would want for nothing more."

"What is it? You can tell us."

"During my life, you put all your wealth at my disposal. Now that I am dying, is there any way I can take some of it with me?"

The couple had no idea how to answer this question. Of course there was no way she could bring anything with her, but they could not bring themselves to say that to their daughter. As they sat there, groping for words, their daughter faded more and more and, finally, drew her last breath.

The couple felt an immense sense of regret for not answering their daughter. How could they have ignored this aspect of life? Because they had been so negligent, when their daughter made her final request, there was nothing they could say to answer her.

If they had regularly listened to the Dharma, surely they could have shared some teachings with their daughter. They now saw their preoccupation with money as detestable. They had thought only of saving money and nothing else. After their daughter's death, they resolved to seek instruction from eminent monastics and learn about the Way. They experienced a sort of rebirth, and went on to become a great philanthropic family.

These young girls were able to teach the Dharma to their parents, and can certainly be seen as manifestations of Avalokitesvara Bodhisattva. There are many times when children can enable their parents to generate the aspiration for enlightenment.

Manifestation as Celestial Beings

For those who should be liberated by someone in such forms as a *deva*, a *naga*, a *yaksa*, a *gandharva*, an *asura*, a *garuda*, a *kimnara*, a *mahoraga*, human or nonhuman being, then he will manifest in all these forms and teach the Dharma to them.

The various manifestations of Avalokitesvara mentioned in this passage are commonly grouped together as the "eight classes of celestial beings." In Chinese the term is rendered as *tianlong babu* (天龍八部), "eight classes of *devas* and *nagas*," since the first two classes are *devas* and *nagas*. The significance of each of these eight classes of celestial beings will be examined one by one:

1. Devas
Devas are god-like beings who inhabit the heavenly realms. All the various deities of the desire realm heavens, the form heavens, and the formless heavens are all considered *devas*. The *Lotus Sutra Commentary* describes *devas* as "Pure and pristinely bright, they are the most honored and supreme, hence the name *deva*."

2. Nagas
Nagas are large, serpent-like waterborne creatures. It is said that they are able to freely make themselves visible to others or remain hidden.

3. Yaksas
Yaksas are demons who are strong, vicious, and usually wicked. They are able to fly through the air for great distances.

4. Gandharvas
Gandharvas are celestial musicians who perform for Lord Sakra. The name "Gandharva" has many meanings, including "perfume seekers," "perfume eaters," "perfume smellers," or "perfume spirits," because they live by consuming perfume vapors. They are found in the Vajra Cave south of Mount Sumeru, and are able to fly through the sky.

5. Asuras

Asuras are similar to *devas*, but less refined. One meaning of the Sanskrit word *asura* is "uncomely" because of their ghastly features, while another meaning is "wine-less," since those who are reborn as *asuras* may have enjoyed wine in previous lives, but are no longer able to drink it.

Those reborn as *asuras* kept the five precepts and practiced the ten wholesome actions in their previous lives, but they were arrogant, jealous, and had a sense of superiority towards others. The *asuras* and the *devas* of Lord Sakra's heaven are constantly at war with one another, and they fight unending battles.

6. Garudas

Garudas are large, bird-like creatures in Indian mythology. In Sanskrit *garuda* means "golden-winged bird," or "wondrously winged bird," to describe its extremely large wingspan of 3,360,000 miles. The *garuda* is also sometimes called the king of birds.

Garudas patrol the four levels of Mount Sumeru and catch *nagas* for food; they wear *mani* pearls—wish-fulfilling jewels—on their heads.

7. Kimnaras

In Sanskrit *Kimnara* means "suspicious human" or "suspicious spirit," for they often manifest in the form of a human being with a single horn on their heads. When people see a *kimnara*, they are often suspicious of them because they look like human beings, but there is something off about them. *Kimnaras* serve Lord Sakra by singing and dancing. Their true form is that of a human body with a horse's head, or a bird's body with a human head.

8. Mahoragas

In Sanskrit, *mahoraga* means "moving on a great belly" or "snake spirit," for they are beings with human bodies but snake heads.

The eight classes of celestial beings described above are all drawn from Indian mythology. The people of India had revered such beings for generations before the Buddha attained enlightenment, and thus the Buddha taught the Dharma in accordance with the capacity of his audience. Buddhism is inclusive of all such deities, and uses them as an opportunity to lead living beings to attain the Way.

Another name for the eight classes of celestial beings in Chinese is *ren feiren deng* (人非人等), "human and non-human beings." This is because some of the beings described above look quite human, like *kimnaras* and *mahoragas*, while there are others, like *nagas*, that look nothing like humans. This goes to show that all human and non-human beings upon the land and in the ocean can all be manifestations of Avalokitesvara Bodhisattva.

Manifestation as Vajrapani

For those who should be liberated by a vajrapani deity, then he will manifest as a vajrapani deity and teach the Dharma to them.

The passage describes Avalokitesvara's manifestation as a vajrapani deity. In Chinese, vajrapani deity is rendered as *zhi jingang shen* (執金剛神), "vajra wielding deity." A *vajra* is an indestructible mace-like weapon from Indian mythology. The vajrapani deity is seen as a protector of Buddhism, and statues of this diety are often placed at the front gate of Buddhist temples.

The *vajra* is known as being extremely dense and firm and as such is a representation of humanity's tenacity. With spiritual firmness we can generate goodness and put an end to delusion; how can we possibly fail when we are driven? If we have the determination of a vajrapani deity, we will be able to break through any difficulty, no matter what it may be.

Avalokitesvara Bodhisattva's Thirty-Three Manifestations

Three Noble Manifestations

1. Buddha
2. *Pratyekabuddha*
3. *Sravaka*

Manifestation as Celestial Kings

4. King Brahma
5. Lord Sakra
6. Isvara
7. Mahesvara
8. Great heavenly general
9. Vaisravara

Manifestation as Human Leaders

10. Lesser king
11. Elder
12. Layperson
13. Minister
14. Brahman

Manifestation as Buddhist Practitioners

15. *Bhiksu*
16. *Bhiksuni*
17. *Upasaka*
18. *Upasika*

Manifestation as Women

19. Female elder
20. Female layperson
21. Female minister
22. Female brahman

Manifestation as Children

23. Young boy
24. Young girl

Manifestation as Celestial Beings

25. *Deva*
26. *Naga*
27. *Yaksa*
28. *Gandharva*
29. *Asura*
30. *Garuda*
31. *Kimnara*
32. *Mahoraga*

Manifestation as Vajrapani Deity

33. Vajrapani Deity

The Scope of Avalokitevara's Manifestations

**Aksayamati, such is the merit that Avalokitesvara
Bodhisattva has accomplished, and the various
forms in which he wanders the various lands bringing liberation to living beings.**

The thirty-three manifestations of Avalokitesvara Bodhisattva listed in the *Universal Gate Sutra* each have their own significance,
but Avalokitesvara's powers are not limited to these thirty-three
manifestations. There is actually no limit to the possible manifestations of Avalokitesvara Bodhisattva.

Long, long ago, Avalokitesvara attained enlightenment as
Zhengfa Ming Tathagata,* and his Dharmakaya pervades all of
this three thousand-fold world system. Having already attained
Buddhahood long ago, Avalokitesvara manifests in a multitude of
forms in response to the thoughts of living beings, manifesting in
whatever form is needed in whatever place. The *Sutra of Golden
Light* states:

> The true Dharmakaya of the Buddha
> Is like the vast open sky,
> Manifesting forms in response to things,
> Just as the sun is reflected in water.

---

* "Tathagata who Clearly Understands the True Dharma."

VII

Offering of the Jeweled Necklace

> This is why all of you should single-mindedly make offerings to Avalokitesvara Bodhisattva, for it is the great Avalokitesvara Bodhisattva who can bestow fearlessness in the midst of terror and in dire circumstances. This is why everyone in this Saha World calls him the bestower of fearlessness.

Having extolled the virtues and skillful means of Avalokitesvara Bodhisattva, in this passage Sakyamuni Buddha encourages the assembly to make offerings to Avalokitesvara Bodhisattva. As in earlier parts of the sutra, the exhortation to make such offerings "single-mindedly" is of great importance. Unless we make offerings single-mindedly, then our energy will dissipate and we will be unable to attain the intercession of Avalokitesvara. But, when our thoughts are focused then our energies will be concentrated and all of our requests will be answered.

The object of our single-minded focus should be the mind of Avalokitesvara Bodhisattva himself. If we continuously recite the name of Avalokitesvara with our speech, contemplate the compassion of Avalokitesvara with our mind, and display reverence and respect with our body, then our verbal, mental, and physical karma will become one with the bodhisattva.

The nature of the "offerings" mentioned in the passage can be variously interpreted. The *Exegesis on the Words and Phrases in the Lotus Sutra* describe the offerings as the physical act of worship, the verbal act of praise, and the mental act of visualizing the Buddha. The sutras make the distinction of "offering in principle" and "offering in practice." Offering in principle is defined as attaining realization by comprehending the principles of the Dharma, while offering in practice includes offerings of incense, flowers, fruit, and other such things presented at a shrine. The best way of making offerings is to combine both principle and practice. By understanding the principles of the Dharma, one will make offerings of incense, flowers, and fruit; and by making offerings of incense, flowers, and fruit one can come to understand the principles of the Dharma. When our offerings in principle and our offerings in practice are consistent, then the mind and body are one, and we will have acted with proper reverence and sincerity.

"Terror" as mentioned in the passage is rendered as *buwei* (怖畏), made up of the characters for "fear" and "dread." "Dire circumstances" is rendered as *jinan* (急難), which refers to urgent disasters. When we find ourselves terrified and confronted with difficulties which we cannot resolve, Avalokitesvara can grant us fearlessness, and we will be able to gain peace of mind.

In the *Suramgama Sutra*, Avalokitesvara Bodhisattva says to Sakyamuni Buddha:

World-Honored One, I further use the Diamond Samadhi and the uncreated sublime power derived from cultivating the practice of hearing, to share with all living beings in the six realms of existence throughout the ten directions and the three time periods, enabling living beings to obtain the virtue of the fourteen kinds of fearlessness from my mind and body.

These fourteen kinds of fearlessness are derivative of Avalokitesvara's great wisdom, great compassion, and great courage. Wisdom allows us to experience the truth of reality, compassion allows us to have extend love universally to ourselves and others, and courage allows us to be victorious in the face of any hardship. With these three virtues, nothing is terrifying in this world. Avalokitesvara enables living beings to attain these virtues, which is why he is called the bestower of fearlessness.

There is also another grouping of gifts within the Buddhist sutras:

1. Gifts of wealth: Giving tangible things.
2. Gifts of Dharma: Giving intangible things like truth or teachings.
3. Gifts of fearlessness: Giving the feeling of material and spiritual security.

We cannot enjoy gifts of wealth or gifts of Dharma without the gift of fearlessness. By offering us the gift of fearlessness, Avalokitesvara allows us to feel peaceful and stable.

Aksayamati Offers the Jeweled Necklace

Aksayamati Bodhisattva said to the Buddha, "World-honored One, now I must make an offering to Avalokitesvara Bodhisattva." Then he took from his neck a necklace of numerous precious gems worth thousands of ounces in gold, and gave it to him saying, "Kind one, accept this necklace of precious gems as a Dharma gift."

Upon hearing the extensive merit and virtues of Avalokitesvara Bodhisattva as Sakyamuni Buddha has described them, Aksayamati Bodhisattva feels moved to make an offering to Avalokitesvara. Ornamental necklaces were not uncommon in India, as people would adorn themselves with necklaces and garlands of varying quality depending upon their status and wealth. In accordance with this custom, Buddhas and bodhisattvas were also adorned with such necklaces.

However, given the themes developed throughout the sutra, we should not view the necklace as a tangible object of gold and silver and inlaid with precious gems. The necklace is instead a symbol for the virtues that Aksayamati Bodhisattva has accumulated over many *kalpas* of practice. The gift being offered is therefore not a gift of wealth, but a gift of Dharma.

The use of jeweled necklaces as metaphors for virtue is common throughout Buddhist literature. The *Necklace of Original Conduct Sutra* says:

> Light is the virtue of a million incalculable eons,
> which becomes a necklace made of light to adorn

> the body of the Buddhas. [...] All bodhisattvas
> employ necklaces of virtue to adorn their two
> kinds of Dharmakaya.

The two kinds of Dharmakaya mentioned in the passage are not actually two separate entities, but are two aspects of the Dharmakaya: the Dharmakaya as principle and the Dharmakaya as wisdom. The Dharmakaya as wisdom refers to what is gained when enlightenment is achieved through spiritual practice, while the Dharmakaya as principle is the aspect of the Buddha which is intrinsically present in all beings. Though everyone is endowed with the Dharmakaya as principle, without spiritual practice we cannot realize it. Alternatively, our ability to attain the Dharmakaya as wisdom is dependent upon the Dharmakaya as principle already being present. When we understand that our attainment of enlightenment and our intrinsic nature are not different, then these two aspects of the Dharmakaya become one.

In the *Vimalakirti Sutra* there is a passage very similar to the episode of the jeweled necklace. Vimalakirti, the central figure of the sutra, was a wise layperson who is often seen as a manifestation of Avalokitesvara. In the *Vimalakirti Sutra* there was a certain wealthy elder named Sudatta who had been conducting a seven-day almsgiving ceremony for all brahmans and monastics, Buddhist and non-Buddhist, as well as the poor, outcasts, orphans, and beggars. This was a great offering of wealth, but Vimalakirti approached Elder Sudatta and instructed him on the great benefits of offering the Dharma. Elder Sudatta was overjoyed, and the teaching purified his mind. To express his gratitude he removed his jeweled necklace and offered it to Vimalakirti. In this way Elder Sudatta was not only showing how the teaching delighted him, but was showing how he renounced his own desire for wealth.

In the *Universal Gate Sutra* Avalokitesvara Bodhisattva has given Aksayamati Bodhisattva a great teaching on how the giving of compassion can be a form of giving the Dharma. Aksayamati offers his jeweled necklace out of a similar sense of gratitude.

Avalokitesvara Accepts the Necklace

At the time, Avalokitesvara Bodhisattva was unwilling to accept it. Aksayamati spoke once more to Avalokitesvara Bodhisattva, "Kind one, accept this necklace as a kindness to us."

Aksayamati Bodhisattva presents his jeweled necklace to Avalokitesvara Bodhisattva, but Avalokitesvara is unwilling to accept it. Why?

Avalokitesvara's initial unwillingness to accept the necklace shows his lack of greed. While most people hope for wealth and honor, Avalokitesvara has no need for such treasures. Even from the perspective of the necklace as a symbol for spiritual virtue, Avalokitesvara already possesses boundless virtue.

In another sense, because all beings are endowed with the priceless treasure of Buddha nature, there is truly nothing to give or receive. All things are one and all things are equal, and for this reason there can be no relative love or hate, or acceptance and rejection. Avalokitesvara wished to demonstrate this principle, and therefore did not initially accept the necklace.

Aksayamati then presents the necklace a second time, entreating Avalokitesvara to "accept this [necklace] as a kindness to us."

When viewed from the perspective of non-duality of self and others, Avalokitesvara did not need to accept the necklace, but as a kindness for all living beings, he can accept it. This is why he finally accepts the necklace.

In Buddhism we often seek to go beyond the relative truth of existence, such as relative distinctions between things. The truth of emptiness states that all things are empty, and all things are equal. But the ultimate truth is a union of these two: moving from existence to emptiness is the path of wisdom, while moving from emptiness to existence is the path of compassion. Avalokitesvara first did not accept the necklace on the basis of wisdom, but finally accepted it out of compassion for the earnest request that he do so.

> **Then the Buddha said to Avalokitesvara Bodhisattva, "Accept this jeweled necklace out of compassion for Aksayamati Bodhisattva, as well as the four groups of Buddhist disciples, the *devas, nagas, yaksas, gandharvas, asuras, garudas, kimnaras, mahoragas,* human or nonhuman beings." Thereupon, Avalokitesvara Bodhisattva accepted the jeweled necklace out of compassion for the four groups of Buddhist disciples, the *devas* and *nagas,* and the human and nonhuman beings, and, dividing it into two parts, presented one part to Sakyamuni Buddha and presented the other part to the stupa of Prabhutaratna Buddha.**

The four groups of Buddhist disciples are *bhiksus, bhiksunis, upasakas,* and *upasikas,* as mentioned in the previous chapter. Also, the *devas, nagas,* and other beings are the same as the eight classes of celestial beings, also mentioned in the previous chapter.

What is pertinent about this passage is Avalokitesvara's behavior after accepting the necklace: he splits it in two parts, presenting one part to Sakyamuni Buddha, and one to the stupa of Prabhutaratna Buddha.

The stupa, which is an ornamental enclosure similar to a pagoda, is described in the tenth chapter of the *Lotus Sutra*, "Seeing the Treasure Stupa." The stupa is described as erupting from the earth and containing a Buddha named Prabhutaratna, which means "abundant treasures" in Sanskrit. Prabhutaratna Buddha exists perennially, having perfected his wisdom and attained enlightenment, while Sakyamuni Buddha has eradicated all afflictions and will enter *nirvana.*

Normally when we talk about the three bodies of the Buddha, Sakyamuni Buddha is described as the Nirmanakaya: a physical manifestation of the Buddha which enters the world to teach the Dharma to living beings. However, in this passage, when grouped with Prabhutaratna Buddha and Avalokitesvara Bodhisattva, Sakyamuni Buddha represents the Sambhogakaya. Their relationship is as follows:

Prabhutaratna:
Dharmakaya, the essence of the Buddha.

Sakyamuni:
Sambhogakaya, the characteristics of the Buddha.

Avalokitesvara:
Nirmanakaya, the manifestations of the Buddha.

This is because, in this sutra, Avalokitesvara undergoes the labor of manifesting in the world to liberate beings, while Sakyamuni Buddha describes Avalokitesvara's noble characteristics.

When the jeweled necklace is presented to Avalokitesvara and he separates it into two parts and offers them to the Buddhas, this can be seen as reinforcing the idea that the three are of one essence.

One important question to ask is, If Avalokitesvara accepted the jeweled necklace as a kindness to the four groups of Buddhist disciples and the eight classes of celestial beings, why did he not separate the necklace and divide it among these classes and groups? Why did he present it to Prabhutaratna Buddha and Sakyamuni Buddha?

Even though Avalokitesvara accepted the jeweled necklace for the sake of others, he wanted these beings to realize the principle of three aspects of the Buddha being one. In fact, all beings have the three aspects of the Buddha within them. The great Chan master Linji once said:

> A single thought shining with the light of purity is the Dharmakaya within your mind. A single thought shining with the light of of non-differentiation is the Sambhogakaya within your mind. A single thought shining with the light of of differentiation is the Nirmanakaya within your mind.

The light of purity is the universal principle of inherent enlightenment. This principle becomes obscured in living beings because of their delusions and discrimination, making them unable to realize this state. The light of non-differentiation is what is able to break through this state. Once non-differentiation is present, we can then benefit living beings according to their given conditions. This is the light of differentiation: using the same differentiations observed in other living beings in order to liberate them. Thus, the light of differentiation represents compassion, while the light of non-differentiation represents wisdom.

The mind is like a mirror. Originally the mirror was clear and bright, like the light of the Dharmakaya, but the pristine mirror has been obscured by the dust of ignorance and affliction. By utilizing wisdom we can wipe away the dust until not a single speck of darkness remains. The act of cleaning the mirror is like the light of the Sambhogakaya. However, if this pristinely clear mirror is not put to use, what then is it good for? Only when the mirror is able to reflect the world with all of its differences does it realize its function. Using the mirror to observe the world is the light of the Nirmanakaya. Thus upon the surface of the mirror appears all the wondrous differences of existence.

In Chinese there is a common Buddhist saying: *zhenkong miaoyou* (真空妙有), "true emptiness and wondrous existence." The two concepts are always present together, just like the combined wisdom and compassion of Avalokitesvara.

Wandering

Aksayamati, it is with such freely exercised spiritual powers that Avalokitesvara Bodhisattva wanders through the Saha World.

In the concluding passage of this section Sakyamuni Buddha returns to Aksayamati Bodhisattva's original question. In describing how

Avalokitesvara Bodhisattva utilizes his powers to liberate sentient beings, the text uses the character *you* (遊), "wander." Often times when we try to be compassionate we do so with a certain sense of reluctance. But bodhisattvas are able to wander in a leisurely and carefree manner; because they have renounced any sense of reward, they can soujurn joyfully and without any reluctance.

VIII

Verses on Avalokitesvara

As discussed earlier, the *Universal Gate Sutra* is made up of a prose section and a verse section. The verses were omitted from the translation Kumarajiva made during the Later Qin dynasty, but were later added during the Sui dynasty by two Northern Indian monks named Jñanagupta and Dharmagupta. The prose section and the verse section now circulate together as a single text.

The verses of the *Universal Gate Sutra* largely repeat the same content as the prose section, but with greater poetic flourish. These verses are called *gathas* in Sanskrit, which was translated as the Chinese character *song* (頌), "to praise or celebrate in song." The verses of the *Universal Gate Sutra* use beautiful language to praise the content of the sutra, and are the equivalent of poetry or song.

Aksayamati's Question in Verse

"World-honored One with all the wonderful signs,
Let me now ask about him once more:
For what reason is this son of the Buddha

Named 'Observing the Sounds of the World'?"
World-honored One with all the wonderful signs
Answered Aksayamati in verse:

The first line, "World-honored One with all the wonderful signs," is
Aksayamati Bodhisattva praising Sakyamuni Buddha. Aksayamati
addresses Sakyamuni with the epithet "World-Honored One," as
he does in the prose section, but in the verse he is additionally
described as possessing "all wonderful signs." The wonderful signs
are a reference to the many virtues of the Buddha, as well as the
"thirty-two marks of excellence and eighty noble characteristics,"
which are said to be a set of physical characteristics common to all
Buddhas, and are a visual representation of their positive karma
accumulated from past lives. There is a poem that expresses the
appearance of the Buddha quite well:

> In heaven above and earth below there is no one
>   like the Buddha;
> Nor can a comparison be made to anyone in the
>   world's ten directions.
> I have seen all that this world has to offer;
> But there is absolutely no one like the Buddha.

The use of the words "once more" in the second line are a reference to the verse section being a repetition of the prose section.
Also, while "son of the Buddha" in the third line specifically refers
to Avalokitesvara in this instance, the term is also more generally
used to all the disciples of the Buddha.

In the verse section Aksayamati asks "for what reason" just as
he does in the prose. However, in the prose section this interpreted

as "why," while in the verse section it is taken to mean "what are the causes and conditions," and Sakyamuni Buddha will go on to explain the causes and conditions that have led Avalokitesvara to earn the name "observing the sounds of the world."

Avalokitesvara's Vow and Practice

You listen now to the practice of Avalokitesvara,
Who well responds to every region.
His great vow is as deep as the sea,
Inconceivable even after many *kalpas*.
Having served Buddhas in the hundreds of
    billions,
He has made a great and pure vow.

While Aksayamati's question is essentially the same as his question in the prose section, Sakyamuni Buddha's response differs in some details. While the prose section is concerned primarily with Avalokitesvara Bodhisattva's powers, the verse section also delves into Avalokitesvara's vows and practice.

Sakyamuni Buddha asks Aksayamati to listen carefully to Avalokitesvara's practice. Strictly speaking, one's practice and one's attainment of realization are not two separate things, but they can be discussed separately so that ordinary beings can learn how to practice.

As mentioned before, the mind is like a pure, bright mirror that has been covered with the dust of ignorance. The bright mirror is a symbol of our inherent enlightenment; in order to clean the mirror and restore it to its original brightness, it must be cleaned through the power of cultivation. This is the initial stage of enlightenment.

For each bit of practice in cleaning the mirror, more of one's inherent enlightenment is revealed. Thus practice and enlightenment are one.

For a being like Avalokitesvara Bodhisattva who has already attained enlightenment, his practice is merely a manifestation of his realization, in the same way that his realization is an application of his practice. So while we may speak of Avalokitesvara's practice, it is not the same as the practice of an ordinary being.

Avalokitesvara is called one "who well responds to every region." "All regions" refers to all worlds in the ten directions. In addition to the different cosmological schemes discussed before, this also includes the Buddha lands of the Dharmakaya, Sambhogakaya, and Nirmanakaya.

Concerning Avalokitesvara's "great vow as deep as the sea," all bodhisattvas take upon themselves the four universal vows:

1.   Living beings are limitless, I vow to liberate them.
2.   Afflictions are endless, I vow to eradicate them.
3.   Teachings are infinite, I vow to learn them.
4.   Buddhahood is supreme, I vow to attain it.

By undertaking the first vow to liberate all living beings, bodhisattvas benefit others. By undertaking the second vow to eradicate all afflictions and the third vow to learn all teachings, bodhisattvas benefit themselves. The fourth vow to attain Buddhahood is brings benefiting others and benefiting oneself together.

In addition to undertaking the four vows, the "great vow" mentioned in the sixth line of the verse is a reference to the ten great vows of Avalokitesvara Bodhisattva. These ten vows are related to but different from the four universal vows, as illustrated by the following chart:

Living beings are limitless, I vow to liberate them.

1. May I quickly liberate all living beings.
2. May I soon attain excellent skillful means.

Afflictions are endless, I vow to eradicate them.

3. May I quickly board the boat of *prajna* wisdom.
4. May I soon cross over the sea of suffering.
5. May I quickly attain morality, meditative concentration, and wisdom.

Teachings are infinite, I vow to learn them.

6. May I quickly realize all teachings.
7. May I soon attain the wisdom eye.

Buddhahood is supreme, I vow to attain it.

8. May I soon ascend the mountain of nirvana.
9. May I quickly realize emptiness as a refuge.
10. May I soon be equal to the Dharmakaya.

Avalokitesvara's vows are as deep as the ocean, such that you could contemplate them endlessly—for "many *kalpas*" and never exhaust one's understanding of them. Not only do they allow us to understand Avalokitesvara's practice, but they also give us a glimpse of the great compassion that exists within ourselves that is able to see and hear the Buddha's teachings in the world every day. When we consider, reflect upon, and study them, we cannot possibly ignore Avalokitesvara's vows, and will wish to experience them as well.

Keep in Mind Avalokitesvara's Powers

Let me briefly tell you:
Hearing his name and seeing his form,
Keeping him unremittingly in mind,
Can eliminate all manner of suffering.

This passage restates a more direct formula of the union of physical, verbal, and mental karma: mentally we should hear the name of Avalokitesvara, physically we should see his image and pay homage to it, and verbally we should recite his name. Our practice of the *Universal Gate Sutra* is incomplete if one of these types of karma is lacking, and we would then no longer be exhibiting single-minded effort in our practice.

What differs in the verse section is the relationship Sakyamuni Buddha describes between the three types of karma. Here he states the mental karma of hearing Avalokitesvara's name and the physical karma of seeing Avalokitesvara's image as constituents to being able to single-mindedly recite his name and relieve suffering.

"Hearing his name" specifically refers to hearing the formula, "I take refuge in the great, compassionate Avalokitesvara Bodhisattva." Once the formula has been heard, one will certainly be able to recite it.

"Seeing his form" refers to offering physical acts of worship and homage to images of Avalokitesvara. Some may think that worshiping an image made of wood or drawn on paper cannot possibly result in any virtue, but this is a great mistake. Consider some stalks of bamboo as an example: they can be made into sandals and worn on the feet, or made into a hat and worn on the head. These same stalks of bamboo can be made into paper and be painted with an image of

Avalokitesvara Bodhisattva. What makes this state of the bamboo worthy of worship? In either case, the bamboo is neither superior nor inferior because of its use, the only difference is the precious state of mind the painted bamboo can offer.

The great Chan master Huangbo once said, "Do not seek the Buddha, do not seek the Dharma, do not seek the Sangha." Only worship performed with such an understanding can be profoundly meaningful, even though such an understanding may not be something that most ordinary people experience.

"Keeping him unremittingly in mind" in the third line means to single-mindedly apply effort, and not to be remiss in one's recitation. The *Ten Line Avalokitesvara Sutra* says:

> Recite Avalokitesvara in the morning, and recite Avalokitesvara in the evening. As each recitation arises from the mind, each recitation remains within the mind.

When one recites the name of Avalokitesvara in this way, it is both keeping him in mind and an act of worship. No matter what time it is, one should ensure that you do not become separated from Avalokitesvara Bodhisattva. There is a saying in Buddhism that one should "Rise each day with the Buddha, and sleep each night holding the Buddha." Put simply, we should act as though we live with Avalokitesvara every day. By having such conviction our physical, verbal, and mental karma will always be centered upon Avalokitesvara, and our karma will naturally transform to be more like the bodhisattva's.

What is meant by the saying, "live together with Avalokitesvara," is that we share everything in common with him. Thus, this body becomes Avalokitesvara's body instead of our own, and this mind becomes Avalokitesvara's mind instead of our own. The Japanese Zen master Dogen once said:

> This single day of life is an estimable life with an estimable human body. Having this mind and body to maintain the practice, we should love and respect them.

Considering these words, it becomes clear why this body, temporary though it may be, is so important. If we see the body as Avalokitesvara, we cannot help but love and respect it. Our feelings of gratitude for cultivating the practice become more heartfelt, and we would not dare to be undisciplined in our cultivation.

With all that has come before, how can we put an end to "all manner of suffering"? If we treat this body as Avalokitesvara's body, then our hands, feet, and mouth become his as well. If that is the case, then our hands will not be able to steal, and our mouths will not be able to curse others. When we join our palms together and recite, "I take refuge in the great, compassionate Avalokitesvara Bodhisattva," we integrate the three types of karma and, by doing so, suffering will naturally be eliminated.

IX

Verses on Dangers

Suppose someone with harmful intent,
Casts you into a great pit of fire;
Keep in mind Avalokitesvara's powers,
And the pit of fire will change into a pond.
Or you are cast adrift upon an immense ocean,
Menaced by dragons, fish, and demons;
Keep in mind Avalokitesvara's powers,
And the waves will not drown you.

The verse section develops into a parallel of the seven calamities and three poisons in the prose section. Like the answer to Aksayamati's question, the teachings in the prose section and the verse section are the same, though some of differences in the details are noteworthy.

The first danger described is equivalent to the calamity of fire, and is largely the same, except rather than describing the flames dissipating the fire is said to "change into a pond." While the result is the same, the image of a pond furthers interpretation of the fire as s symbol of anger: when anger is relieved one is cool, refreshed, and placid.

The next danger corersponds to the calamity of flood, but in the verse section it describes a person drowning and being menaced by sea creatures. The "immense ocean" is the great ocean of afflictions, and the dragons, fish, and demons represent love and desire. That being said, the body of a temptress can be more terrible than dragons or fish, and the bewitching charms of beauty can be more frightful than evil demons! If at such times we can apply the wisdom of Avalokitesvara and realize that all phenomena are merely a temporary combination of cause and conditions, then the confusion and attachment to love and desire will come to an end.

The Danger of Falling

Or someone pushes you down,
From the top of Mount Sumeru;
Keep in mind Avalokitesvara's powers,
And you will hang in the sky like the sun.
Or you are pursued by evil doers,
Who push you down from Mount Vajra;
Keep in mind Avalokitesvara's powers,
And not one of your hairs will be harmed.

The two dangers described in this passage occupy the same space as the calamity of wind storms in the prose section, though the verse section is completely different. Both describe invoking Avalokitesvara to save one from falling from a great height.

Since we all have the potential to become Buddhas because of our inherent Buddha nature, there are some people who derive from this teaching a sense of arrogance. They may think, "Since I have Buddha nature, what is so special about this Sakyamuni person, or this Bodhidharma fellow?" These arrogant, prideful thoughts are self-destructive, and others will be quick to knock you down a peg.

But if we can maintain the universally compassionate mind of Avalokitesvara Bodhisattva, then we will not insult others. If we can maintain the great courage of Avalokitesvara, we will give ourselves encouragement, and ascend as high as the sun hanging in the sky, gliding across the open sky and over the vast ocean.

"Mount Sumeru" is known as being extremely tall, and as such is a metaphor for Buddha nature. "Mount Vajra" can literally be translated as "indestructible," and is a metaphor for faith. Taking a slightly more complicated and technical approach, each of the mountains can be seen as representing different stages in a bodhisattva's development, with Mount Sumeru representing wondrous enlightenment and Mount Vajra representing equal enlightenment.

When we have established faith, we must then make it stable such that it can persist even when we are surrounded by temptation and intimidation. The "evil doers" described in the fifth line are those factors that seek to push us away from our faith. By recollecting the courage of Avalokitesvara Bodhisattva, we can remain unmoved by temptation and intimidation, and remain free and at ease, unharmed.

In Buddhism to be unshakable in this way is often called being "unmoved by the eight winds." In a conventional sense the Chinese term *bafeng* (八風), "eight winds," can refer to the winds of the four cardinal directions and the four intermediate directions. However, in a Buddhist content the eight winds are eight factors that can alter and effect our behavior. They are as follows:

1. Gain: Moments that benefit you, or when things go as you wish.
2. Loss: Everything diminishing, or moments when you are disappointed or frustrated.
3. Defamation: Being maligned by others behind your back.
4. Honor: Having others express their admiration to you.
5. Praise: Being held in esteem by others.
6. Ridicule: Being despised by others.
7. Sorrow: Experiencing the painful effects of negative karma.
8. Joy: Experiencing the pleasurable effects of positive karma.

Each of the eight winds can have a profound effect upon our minds and our faith. But if we can strengthen our faith such that nothing outside of us can alter it, then even if vast riches are placed in front of us, we can maintain our integrity, and even having a knife at our throats will not change our principles.

The Danger of Execution

Or if surrounded by malevolent brigands,
Each one brandishing a knife to attack you;
Keep in mind Avalokitesvara's powers,
And they will all experience a sense of
     compassion.
Or if persecuted by the royal court,

Facing death by execution;
Keep in mind Avalokitesvara's powers,
And the executioner's blade will break into pieces.

The first four lines of this passage is parallel to the calamity of brigands, though it is presented in an abbreviated form. Lines five through eight are parallel to the passage on the calamity of weapons, though the circumstances in the verse section are very different: here the weapon mentioned is the blade of the executioner, being wielded by the state.

During the past ages of despotic rule, it was not uncommon for the law to simply be the favor of the king, and a violation of that law could mean death. The passage describes the weapon of an executioner falling apart when impacting one who keeps Avalokitesvara in mind. There is indeed a legend regarding the Japanese monastic Nichiren, who was to be executed at the Tatsunokuchi execution grounds. He is supposed to have said, "If I could exchange this ugly head of mine for the *Lotus Sutra*, how truly happy I would be!" and the executioner was unable to do him any harm.

The laws of the state should be obeyed, but as these laws were made by human beings, they sometimes must be changed. The law should not be considered complete or perfect. That being said, even if the law is imperfect, it still has power, and anyone who breaks the law will not be able to escape punishment.

During the age of despotic rule, the law's adjudicator was both the leader of the state and the enforcer the law. This caused great injustice, such as in the case of the twelfth-century Chinese general Yue Fei. Yue Fei famously met his death because his enemy at court uttered the words, "there's no need," when asked for proof of Yue Fei's crimes. How is the law to judge when the person enforcing it is himself a lawbreaker? This is one of the imperfections of the legal system.

The philosopher Socrates took the cup of poison without the slightest sense of fear, and calmly went to his death. Jesus perished upon the cross like the falling of dew. Examples such as these from all times and from all over the world are truly numerous.

Just before his death, the fourteenth-century Samurai Kusunoki Masashige wrote five Chinese characters on a banner: *fei li fa quan tian* (非理法權天), "irrationality, reason, law, power, and heaven." The five characters are written in order from weakest to strongest: irrationality cannot overcome reason, reason cannot overcome law, law cannot overcome power, and power cannot overcome heaven. In this instance "heaven" means the truth of the universe, for no matter how powerful one is the universe is still the ultimate victor. This universal truth is similar to the Dharmakaya. Even when the physical body comes to an end, the Dharmakaya can never end.

The Danger of Spells and Poison

Or if imprisoned with cangue and chains,
Hands and feet manacled and shackled;
Keep in mind Avalokitesvara's powers,
And the bonds will loosen and you will be
    liberated.
If there is someone who would do you harm,
Using spells and various poisons;
Keep in mind Avalokitesvara's powers,
And any harm will rebound on the originator.

The first four lines of the passage are substantially the same as the calamity of imprisonment as described in the prose section. Lines five through eight are unique to the verse section, and describe the danger of spells and poison.

Spells are rendered in Chinese as *zhouzu* (咒詛), "curses," though this includes all manner of occult behavior that seeks to harm others, including calling upon evil spirits, making straw figures and inserting pins into them, or drawing magical symbols and setting them on fire. *Duyao* (毒藥), "poison," refers to any substance that can harm the body when ingested. The passage mentioned that if either of these dangers beset one who keeps Avalokitesvara's powers in mind, the spells and poisons will rebound and be inflicted upon the aggressors.

Who of us can say that we are completely free of the mindset that wishes to harm others? Very few people are completely devoid of jealous tendencies. It can be as subtle as feeling the need to interject a few words of criticism when someone is successful or praised by others. One may feel glad when seeing others fail, or even laugh derisively and think, "Serves them right!" Such feelings of jealousy are not unlike the mindset of someone who would seek to harm another through spells or poison. In fact, it could be said that isolating or wounding others is far worse than any poison.

When we try to inflict harm on others by "casting spells," who is it that ends up with the negative karmic effects? Undoubtably the person wishing to do harm. It is just like presenting someone with a gift: if they are unwilling to accept the gift, the gift still belongs to you. If you try to curse someone but they do nothing to you in return and do not accept your curses, do they not rebound back to you?

In our daily lives there are surely people who are jealous of us and would attempt to hurt us. We should not be shaken in the slightest by such conditions; we should abide in our faith of universal compassion, and cultivate the patience to bear adversity. The Buddha said it best in the *Sutra in Forty-Two Sections*:

> When bad people try and harm the worthy, it is like spitting up at the sky: The spittle does not reach the sky, but falls back upon oneself. Or it is like throwing dirt against the wind; the dirt does not reach the others, but comes back to dirty one's own body. The worthy cannot be harmed, while misfortune will certainly destroy oneself.

The Danger of Wicked Beasts and Poisonous Creatures

Or if you encounter evil *raksas*,
Venomous dragons, various ghosts, and the like;
Keep in mind Avalokitesvara's powers,
And then none of them will dare harm you.
If you are surrounded by evil beasts
With their sharp teeth and claws so horrifying;
Keep in mind Avalokitesvara's powers,
And they will flee in all directions.
When lizards, snakes, vipers, and scorpions
Scorch you with their poisonous vapors;
Keep in mind Avalokitesvara's powers,
And they will retreat at the sound of your voice.
When thunderclouds rumble with lighting strikes,

As hailstones and torrential rains come down;
Keep in mind Avalokitesvara's powers,
And the storm will disperse that very moment.

The first four lines of the passage are substantially the same as the calamity of evil spirits from the prose section. The evil spirits mentioned in the verse section are once again symbols of our various afflictions. What is important to remember is that we can only become enlightened because these afflictions exist in the first place. One of the foundations of Mahayana Buddhism is that afflictions themselves are enlightenment. It is for this reason that sudden enlightenment is even possible. The only thing that makes our afflictions afflictions, not enlightenment, is our obsessed attachment to the self.

From the idea of self arises all manner of distinctions. When we create a distinction between this being my child and that being your child, we create love, hate, a sense of partiality. When we create a distinction between this being my thing and that being your thing, we create greed and miserliness. However, if we can open and expand ourselves, then all living beings become our children and everything belongs to us. In this way we can develop a sense of fairness and equality, and what were once afflictions will become enlightenment itself. Just as the sharp astringent taste of a persimmon becomes sweet in the end, so too do our afflictions become enlightenment when they are awash in the compassionate light of the Buddha.

The dangers of the "evil beasts" and "lizards, snakes, vipers, and scorpions" are an extension of the calamity of evil spirits. The "evil beasts" represent our major afflictions, while the poisonous creatures represent our minor afflictions. Minor afflictions should not be ignored, for as the *Dharmpada says:*

Though drops of water are small, they can slowly fill a large vessel; great wickedness originally
does not start out big, but accumulates from small
things. If you do not ignore minor wickedness,
then you will avoid disaster.

The last four lines of the passage describe the danger of a thun-
derstorm. In this image, the intrinsic mind is like a clear blue sky
that is slowly filled with the swirling dark clouds of delusion. The
small dark clouds of differentiation gather and soon grow into a
storm with the thunderous roar of rage, electricity of greed, light-
ning strike of anger, and torrential rains of self-despair. It is my
thinking of the powers of Avalokitesvara that the clouds disperse
and the rains stops, making everything pure and clear once again.

In all of the dangers mentioned, the key phrase to transform
is to "keep in mind Avalokitesvara's powers." Our own powers are
relatively limited, while the powers of Avalokitesvara are universal. The ability to turn this mind so attached to partialities and rela-
tiveness towards universality and absoluteness is the foundation of
Buddhism.

Liberation from Suffering

Living beings suffer in agony,
Oppressed by immeasurable pain;
The power of Avalokitesvara's wondrous wisdom
Can bring liberation from the world's sufferings.

The previous passages of the verse section are called the "twelve
dangers," and roughly correspond to the seven calamities from the

prose section. In the prose section, these are followed by passages on the three poisons and the two wishes which represent some of the internal qualities that Avalokitesvara can act upon, in contrast to the seven calamites which are all external dangers. In the verse section, these internal qualities are all encapsulated in the four lines mentioned above: the suffering of all living beings.

All living beings suffer, because all living beings have the three poisons of greed, anger, and ignorance. These are most pronounced in the first six realms of existence, but even bodhisattvas, *pratyeka-buddhas*, and *sravakas* are affected by minute quantities of the three poisons. Only Buddhas have removed them in their entirety.

Among these six realms of existence the poison of anger is most severe in the hell realm, the poison of greed is most severe in the realm of hungry ghosts, and the poison of ignorance is most severe in the animal realm. The poison of anger is more mildly pronounced but still most prominent in the *asura* realm, just as greed is present in the human realm, and ignorance in the heavenly realm.

Even though humans have less greed and desire when compared with hungry ghosts, the instances of pain and suffering fomented by such desire and greed are more numerous than the grains of sands in the Ganges River. Among all these types of suffering, birth, old age, sickness, and death are the most significant. Also prominent are the sadness of being apart from loved ones, the aggravation of being near loathsome people, the despair of being unable to obtain what we want, and the intense suffering of the five aggregates.

Avalokitesvara's wondrous power of wisdom can liberate us from the suffering of this world. Suffering comes from our negative physical, verbal, and mental karma, which we create because of our own lack of wisdom. In order to end our delusion, we must stop producing negative karma. In Buddhist repentance ceremonies, the following verse is chanted to this effect:

> The numerous negative karmas
> > created in the past,
> All stem from beginning-less greed, anger,
> > and ignorance
> Generated by my body, speech, and mind;
> I now repent of them all entirely.

X

Verses on Virtues

In Praise of the Three Karmas

Perfect in supernatural powers,
Widely practicing the skillful means of wisdom,
In all the lands of the ten directions,
There is no place where he fails to manifest.
The lower realms in all their forms,
That of hell-beings, hungry ghosts, and animals,
The sufferings of birth, old age, sickness, and death,
He steadily brings them all to an end.

This passage in the verse section is parallel to the thirty-three manifestations in the prose section. Rather than listing each of the manifestations of Avalokitesvara Bodhisattva, the verse section offers several succinct expressions of Avalokitesvara's essence, function, and form.

The essence of Avalokitesvara is his wondrous wisdom power, as discussed in the previous chapter. The function of Avalokitesvara is his ability to employ supernatural powers and skillful means. In the first line Avalokitesvara is described as "perfect in supernatural powers." Both Buddhas and bodhisattvas are said to possess certain supernatural powers born from their great wisdom. There are six types of supernatural powers mentioned throughout the Buddhist sutras, which are as follows:

1. Teleportation: The ability to pass through any impediment instantaneously.
2. Celestial vision: The ability to see things beyond one's range of vision.
3. Celestial hearing: The ability to hear things beyond one's range of hearing.
4. Mind reading: The ability to know the thoughts of others.
5. Knowledge of past lives: The ability to recall all the details of one's past lives.
6. Destruction of all afflictions: Having ended one's afflictions.

"Widely practicing the skillful means of wisdom" is another reference to the multiplicity and variety of skillful means employed by Avalokitesvara in order to liberate sentient beings.

The form of Avalokitesvara is his many manifestations. In the above passage the manifestations are expressed in terms of the many different locations he manifests, as in the line "all the lands of the ten directions," which is equivalent to everywhere.

Truth pervades the universe, and Avalokitesvara can manifest anywhere. For example, James Watt observed something as simple as steam coming from a kettle and discovered steam power. A kite string was what led Benjamin Franklin to realize the existence of electricity. Sir Isaac Newton came to understand the force of gravity because an apple fell from a tree. The flowers and grasses of the open countryside provide the poet with literary inspiration, and the moon fixed amid the pine trees makes the traveler think of home. The sight of destitute beggars engenders a sense of compassion, and upon seeing someone old and infirm, we sense the impermanence of the world. All of these are manifestations of Avalokitesvara.

"The lower realms in all their forms," specifically refers to the hell realm, the realm of hungry ghosts, and the animal realm, while the "sufferings of birth, old age, sickness, and death" are the four sufferings of human life. Each of these are slowly eliminated by Avalokitesvara.

Such words imply that there is some external thing that acts upon us, but this is not the case. The Buddhas and bodhisattvas teach us that if we wish to attain liberation, we can do so through applying our own wisdom to come to an understanding of the true reality of phenomena. This is the only way that rebirth in these lower realms will be ended and their suffering eliminated. There is a saying in Buddhism: "Everyone in every way is Avalokitesvara/a lifetime for each person on his sacred Mount Putuo." We should realize that Avalokitesvara is not some other person, but is how we should cultivate ourselves to be. This is very important.

The Five Contemplations

Contemplation of truth, contemplation of purity,
Contemplation of the vast and greater wisdom,
Contemplation of compassion and contemplation
 of kindness;
Ever longed for, ever looked up to.

His undefiled light of purity
Is the wisdom-sun dispelling all darkness,
What can quell winds and fires that bring disaster
And illuminate the world universally.

The first three lines from this passage include what are known as the five contemplations. The character in Chinese for "contemplation" is *guan* (觀), which is the same character used in *guanshiyin*, the Chinese translation of Avalokitesvara's name. Each of the five contemplations are derivative of Avalokitesvara's power of wisdom such that, even though the five are distinct, they are all tied together by Avalokitesvara's wisdom. Buddhist tradition has often analyzed the contemplations of truth, purity, and wisdom as representing emptiness, skillful means, and the Middle Way, the combination of both. But this is not the only possible interpretation.

The following five contemplations are what allow Avalokitesvara Bodhisattva to be as he is, and are derivative of both his fundamental and acquired wisdom. In other words, even though Avalokitesvara was able to reside in *nirvana*, due to his aspiration to liberate living beings he created this fivefold division of his wondrous abilities.

The Contemplation of Truth

The contemplation of truth is the wisdom of Avalokitesvara's enlightenment, and could also possibly be called the "contemplation of wisdom." Chan Master Huangbo Xiyun wrote in the *Essential Teachings of Mind Transmission*:

The nature of enlightenment is as eternal as space itself since beginningless time. It has never been created nor has it ever been destroyed. It has never existed nor has it ever not existed. It has never been contaminated nor has it ever been purified. It has no location, no dimension, no number, no shape, no form, and no sound. It cannot be grasped using language nor can it be comprehended by experiential phenomena. All the Buddhas, bodhisattvas, and all beings with sentience share this quality, for this is the inherent nature of great *nirvana.*

The inherent nature of *nirvana* is the contemplation of the truth of enlightenment, and the contemplation of the truth of enlightenment is the inherent nature of *nirvana.*

The Contemplation of Purity

The contemplation of purity describes how one realizes the inherent purity of the mind after the contemplation of truth has been perfected. With such contemplation all phenomena can appear before you undefiled. The *Complete Enlightenment Sutra* states:

Since the mind is pure, the perception of objects is pure; and since the perception of objects is pure, the eye sense-organ is pure... so the same follows as well for the nose, tongue, body, and mind. Good man, since the [eye] sense-organ is pure, the visual sense object is pure; and since the visual sense object is pure, so too is the sound sense object pure. This same holds for the sense objects of smell, taste, touch, and phenomena.

When the sequence mentioned above is extended the four great elements, all the sense organs, objects and consciousnesses, and even the entirety of the universe can become completely pure and completely enlightened. This is Avalokitesvara's contemplation of purity.

The Contemplation of the Vast and Greater Wisdom

Having contemplated living beings from the perspective of the contemplation of truth and the contemplation of purity, one can then contemplate the vast and greater wisdom, and seek to liberate these beings from one's unconditioned compassion. This is great wisdom, and is a natural byproduct of the previous contemplations.

The compassion that arises from a bodhisattva who contemplates the vast and greater wisdom is different from other kinds of compassion. This compassion is known as "unconditioned compassion," and is the compassion of Mahayana Buddhism and of the bodhisattva path. The lesser form of compassion, the compassion of the provisonal Buddhist teachings, is that of "afflicted compassion."

The *Vimalakirti Sutra* illustrates the difference between unconditioned compassion and afflicted compassion. In the sutra, Buddhas and living beings are described as one and the same. There are some who believe that living beings are deluded by the cycle of birth and death and are not peers of the Buddha in any way. This distinction generates false views about the permanence of existence and what is beneficial, and as such these ideas are regarded with contempt in the *Vimalakirti Sutra*.

Muso Soseki, one of Japan's fourteenth-century national masters, offered an apt analogy to clarify the distinction between unconditioned compassion and afflicted compassion: We often see beggars out begging along the streets and alleyways. Some of these were originally from poor families and have lived in poverty since childhood. There are others who were originally born into wealthy families that were later reduced to poverty owing to various circumstances. We can observe that among these two kinds of beggars, the ones that were originally born into wealthy families experience a sense of pity more easily, which is greater than what we can see among those beggars who originally came from poor families. This is like the compassion of true bodhisattvas who know that all living beings share the same essence with the Buddhas and are free of the marks of the cycle of birth and death. They know that living beings acquire the marks of the cycle of birth and death with the arising of a single ignorant thought where none originally existed. Such marks of are as unreal as a dream or an illusion.

This is where the bodhisattva who only understand provisional truth differ: they view living being like those beggars who have been born into poverty. They believe that living beings truly wallow in the cycle of birth and death and thus they generate afflicted compassion. This is how the unconditioned compassion of a true bodhisattva is different.

Avalokitesvara has already experienced enlightenment, so when he looks upon living beings with the contemplation of the truth and the contemplation of purity, he can see them as one with the Buddha. He is like a beggar who was formerly of a wealthy family, but was reduced to poverty because of a single slip—he cannot help but have unconditioned compassion. For one who has unconditioned compassion, the cycle of birth and death is not the cycle of birth and death and affliction is not affliction, just as one vows to liberate sentient beings even though there are no sentient beings to liberate.

Once someone asked Chan Master Huangbo Xiyun, "How do all the Buddhas practice great loving-kindness and compassion? How do they teach the Dharma to living beings?"

Chan Master Huangbo replied, "All the Buddhas practice loving-kindness and compassion because they are unconditioned. That is why it is called great loving-kindness and compassion. Loving-kindness should not be seen as something the Buddhas can fulfill; nor should compassion be seen as something that can liberate living beings. As for the Dharma they teach, there is no teaching or instruction; and as for those who request the Dharma, there is no request or attainment. It is like an illusory master teaching the Dharma to an illusory audience."

When viewed in this way, all living beings are one with each other. There is no one to liberate and no one to attain anything. It is only because people wandered away from home in confusion that teaching the Dharma becomes a way for them to return home. Thus, only listening to the Dharma for the purpose of liberating living beings can constitute the bodhisattva's contemplation of the vast and greater wisdom.

The Contemplation of Compassion and Kindness

These two other contemplations are derived from the contemplation of the vast and greater wisdom. The contemplation of compassion is removing the suffering of living beings. The contemplation of kindness is bestowing living beings with the joy of the contemplation of truth and of purity, thus enabling them to return to oneness with the Buddha. These forms of compassion and kindness are in accord with the unconditioned compassion mentioned earlier.

Avalokitesvara is "ever longed for [and] ever looked up to" because he possess both fundamental and acquired wisdom, and has perfected his ability to benefit himself and others. Thus we long for him to bestow upon us liberation, and we look up to his virtue.

The description "his undefiled light of purity is the wisdom-sun dispelling all darkness" summarizes the qualities of the five contemplations. It is also the same as one of the descriptions of the twelve lights in the *Sutra on the Buddha of Infinite Life*.

The phrase "what can quell winds and fires that bring disaster" is a reference to the disasters mentioned previously. The disaster of flood should likely be included, and was probably only left out because of its inability to fit within the poetic form of the five-character line used within the sutra. "Illuminate the world universally" describes the scope of Avalokitesvara's light, extending all over the earth, describing it as capable of eradicating all darkness.

The darkness mentioned in the passage is a symbol for the afflictions which obscure the brightness of the mind. By removing the winds of ignorance and affliction, the fires of greed and anger, and the floods of desire and attachment, the brightness of the mind can become completely uncontaminated. When our minds shine with the light of wisdom, we realize the mistakes we had made in the past and understand that our current state is how things should have been all along.

Teaching and Fearlessness

**Precepts of his compassionate body are
    like rolling thunder;
The profundity of his kind mind is
    like a great cloud;**

> He showers us with Dharma rain like nectar,
> That extinguishes the flames of affliction.

This passage praises the way that Avalokitesvara teaches the Dharma, and though this act would be categorized as verbal karma, we should consider it in conjunction with all three types of karma. In addition to the verbal karma of teaching the Dharma, the kindness and expansiveness "like a great cloud" is the teacher's mental karma, and his moral and dignified conduct is the teacher's physical karma.

The essence of compassion is the removal of suffering. Avalokitesvara saw living beings mired in pain and suffering because of their negative karma, and generated a mind of great compassion to ensure that all living beings know how to prevent wrongdoing. His guidance is as vigorous as rolling thunder, able to support and subdue all that is wrong and unwholesome.

Kindness is the ability to give happiness to all living beings. Avalokitesvara is not great only because he removes suffering, but he also bestows happiness upon living beings: "He showers us with Dharma rain like nectar." "Nectar" is a symbol of the truth of the Dharma, for only the Dharma is capable of extinguishing the flames of affliction.

If we too have this vigorous spirit to remove suffering and have such compassion that we bestow happiness on all living beings the fires of our own afflictions will be extinguished.

> When lawsuits bring you to court,
> Or when fear strikes you in battle,
> Keep in mind Avalokitesvara's powers,
> And the enemy forces will all retreat.

This next passage is parallel to the description of Avalokitesvara's bestowal of fearlessness in the prose section. If one keeps in mind the powers of Avalokitesvara Bodhisattva, then one can be fearless when entering a court of law, facing soldiers on the battlefield, being beset by the seven calamities, or threatened by the three poisons.

The "lawsuits" mentioned in the first line can be read as more widely refering to all manner of disputes and arguments. The ignorance and affliction of our mind is like a constant battle. If we keep in mind Avalokitesvara's powers, the enemy will retreat. If we remember the five contemplations of Avalokitesvara we will have nothing to fear.

The Five Voices

Contemplating the world's voices with a
    wondrous voice,
A Brahma voice, an ocean-tide voice,
What surpasses those voices of the world;
Therefore constantly keep them in mind.

This passage includes what are known as the "five voices," called *yin* (音), which is also a component of *guanshiyin*. While the five contemplations are subjective qualities that include things like contemplations, visualizations, and observations, the five voices are objective, and denote what is experienced by others.

Though the five voices specifically refer to what is heard, these qualities are not limited only to hearing. "Wondrous voice" could also include wondrous sight, wondrous smell, wondrous taste, wondrous touch, or wondrous thought. However, as has been mentioned before, hearing is of special significance to Avalokitesvara, and that is why it is discussed here.

The "wondrous voice" and "contemplating the world's voices" both partake of the union of existence and emptiness expressed in the contemplation of the vast and greater wisdom. The substantial difference between the two is that the wondrous voice communicates the Middle Way by means of emptiness, while contemplating the world's voices communicates the Middle Way by means of existence. Another way to look at it is to say that the wondrous voice points upward while contemplating the world's voices points downward. The two are different, but their result is the same.

One who appreciates the essence of the *Lotus Sutra* hears every gust of wind over a mountain peak and every rippling wave as a wondrous sound, as well as the sound of every business dealing. Avalokitesvara is able to observe all such sounds and hear those who call his name, bring aid to their suffering and misery, and liberate them.

The "Brahma voice" means that both the mundane and supramundane teachings spoken by the bodhisattva are pure and undefiled, and that all teachings are established on the basis of the contemplation of purity. "What surpasses those voices of the world" means surpassing worldly distinctions and establishing oneself in the contemplation of the truth. This means that what the bodhisattva sees and hears is treated with absolute impartiality, the application of which becomes the contemplation of kindness and the contemplation of compassion.

The bodhisattva uses kindness and compassion to bring liberation to the world with consistency like the tidewaters of the ocean: never pausing for a moment, the bodhisattva is always in motion, responding to any given time and place. Sometimes ebbing, sometimes flowing, the bodhisattva acts freely. This is the "ocean-tide voice."

These five voices can be seen as different notes on a musical scale. Though each one is different, this perception merely arises from differences in order: first or last, left or right. Actually, all of these voices are the same. Objectively, the five voices are the sound of the truth of the universe. Subjectively, they are the sounds which innately exist within our minds. They are not sounds which are heard by the ear, but rather are heard by the mind. They are not seen by the eyes; they are seen in the mind. These latent voices within the mind become Avalokitesvara's five voices for us to remember and reflect upon.

Doubt and Worship

Never doubt from moment to moment,
The pure and noble Avalokitesvara;
For those in pain and agony, or facing death,
He can be their aid and support!

Having described the virtues of Avalokitesvara in various ways, in this passage Sakyamuni Buddha entreats the audience not to doubt. The passage begins, "never doubt from moment to moment," to encourage people to have faith. This is similar to the passage "the Dharma is like a great ocean, but only the faithful can enter it," discussed earlier. If you do not believe, no matter how precious a particular form of practice there may be, you would still be unable to receive and follow it.

"Moment to moment" refers to all our thoughts from the past to the future. Sometimes when we first learn something we may have faith in it for awhile, but before long we become doubtful again and return to our previous beliefs. In the passage Sakyamuni Buddha says that faith in one moment and doubt in the next will not work. We must maintain our faith from moment to moment in order for there to be any results.

Chan Master Daoyuan once said, "When faith is realized, Buddhahood is realized." Religions are established on the basis of faith, and all great strength is built upon faith. This differs from intellectual learning that makes doubt its starting point. But, when put in these terms, doesn't it seem like religion is opposed to intellectual learning? Not at all. Religion establishes its principles above those of intellectual learning, and it puts its faith where intellectual learning cannot reach. Religion is not against intellectual learning at all, but rather transcends it. By and large Buddhism is highly rational, but it must also attend to the broad demands of feeling and sentiment and create a place for spiritual security. This place of security is the foundation of faith. Like a mother or father, Avalokitesvara helps and supports living beings amidst their pain, agony, and fears of death.

> **In possession of all merit and virtue,**
> **He views living beings with compassionate eyes;**
> **His ocean of accumulated merit is infinite,**
> **So worship him with prostrations.**

Avalokitesvara Bodhisattva is the pure and noble liberator of the world who manifests in the form of a bodhisattva. The merit and virtue of Avalokitesvara are incalculable, though there are three virtues that should be specifically mentioned: the virtue of the Dharmakaya, the virtue of *prajna*, and the virtue of liberation.

One attains the virtue of the Dharmakaya by contemplating the truth of emptiness, one attains the virtue of *prajna* through contemplating the truth of existence, and one attains the virtue of liberation by contemplating the truth of the Middle Way.

This process can be explained in another way: eliminating affliction by contemplating the truth of emptiness and becoming free of attachments is the virtue of eliminating affliction. Applying wisdom by contemplating the truth of existence to adapt to all differentiations is the virtue of wisdom. Applying oneself to the Middle Way unhindered is the virtue of application. The virtue of eliminating affliction, the virtue of wisdom, and the virtue of application can also be called the three virtues.

Avalokitesvara fully possesses all merit and virtue, and views all living beings with compassionate eyes. As a consequence of this merit and virtue, he possesses limitless blessings, and all living beings are able to partake of his blessings and wisdom. His merit, blessings, and wisdom are like the water in the great ocean: they neither increase nor decrease, and are immeasurable. Living beings make this the foundation for their spirit, and having entrusted their lives to Avalokitesvara they pay homage to him with prostrations as a way of expressing their gratitude for his kindness. How could they not?

In addition to seeking out the Avalokitesvara that is outside of us and possesses such immeasurable merit and virtue, we must think of what is inside ourselves. The Tathagatagarbha, the origin of the Buddha that is inherently endowed with inexhaustible merit and virtue, lies within our minds. But merit and virtue cannot manifest if the doors to the Tathagatagarbha are closed. The eighth-century monastic Master Jingxi Zhanran made this poignant comment:

It is sad that the matrix of mysteries [the
Tathagatagarbha] does not manifest because it
is obscured by the three delusions. Thus the delusion of ignorance shrouds the Dharma nature,
the delusion regarding phenomena as numerous
as grains of sand blocks spiritual transformation,
and the delusions to be eliminated in the paths
of seeing and cultivation hinder the tranquil state
of *nirvana*. However, in essence, these three delusions are unreal fabrications.

Experiencing how ignorance is an unreal fabrication and illu-
minating the Dharma nature is the contemplation of the vast and
greater wisdom. The grains of sand mentioned in the quote above
are a metaphor for the many ways that we remain unaware, and
eliminating these so that we can experience spiritual transformation is the contemplation of purity. Removing the delusions of the
path that come from attachments to differentiation and revealing
the tranquility of *nirvana* is the contemplation of truth.

In revealing the Tathagatagarbha we become completely
endowed with all merit and virue, and then view living beings
through the contemplations on compassion and kindness. This is
how one reveals Avalokitesvara's accumulated blessings, merit,
and virtue in one's own mind.

A man named Ji Zong who lived in China during the Liu Song
dynasty once asked a monk from India, "What is Avalokitesvara
chanting with the rosary he holds in his hands?"

The monk replied, "He is chanting the name of
Avalokitesvara."

"But why would he want to chant his own name?" Ji Zong asked further.

"It is better to help yourself than to seek help from others!"

This meaning behind this dialogue is the same reason that we pay homage to Avalokitesvara with prostrations.

Sanskrit Verses

The Sanskrit version of the *Universal Gate Sutra* features some additional verses which are not found in Jñanagupta and Dharmagupta's translation. They are provided below:

> Bringing liberation to the world with compassion,
> He will attain true enlightenment in the future,
> And destroy the pain of worry and fear.
> So pay homage to Avalokitesvara with prostrations.
> When Amitabha Buddha was the Bhiksu Dharmakara,
> First among the disciples of Lokesvararaja Buddha,
> He cultivated the practice for hundreds of eons,
> And attained unsurpassed pure enlightenment.
> Avalokitesvara was always in attendance,
> Keeping Amitabha Buddha cool with a fan,
> He displays the magical powers of samadhi,
> And makes offerings to all the Buddhas.
> The Pure Land in the West,
> Is the Land of Ultimate Bliss,
> Where Amitabha Buddha now abides,
> Becoming the Tamer of Sentient beings.
> In that land there are no women,
> Nor can any impure phenomena be seen.

Sons of Buddhas now seek rebirth there,
And enter the lotus matrix.
That Buddha of immeasurable light,
Upon the pure and profound dais of lotuses,
Emits hundreds of light beams from the lion throne,
Just like King Salendra.
Such a World-Honored One,
Is unparalleled among the three realms;
Pay homage to and praise him to accumulate merit,
And quickly become a most excellent person.

XI

Transmission

At this time Dharanimdhara Bodhisattva rose from his seat, came forward, and said to the Buddha, "World-honored One, if there are living beings who hear this chapter on Avalokitesvara Bodhisattva about his freedom of action, his revelation of the universal gate, and his supernatural powers, it should be known that their merits are not few."

At the conclusion of the laudatory verse, there is a brief prose section that closes the *Universal Gate Sutra* and shows the transmission of the teachings of the sutra. As Sakyamuni Buddha finished answering Aksayamati Bodhisattva's question, Dharanimdhara Bodhisattva rose from his seat among the assembly and praised the merit of the teaching just delivered.

Dharanimdhara Bodhisattva, whose Chinese name is *chidi* (持地) "earth holder," is generally understood as another name for Ksitigarbha Bodhisattva, whose Chinese name is *dizang* (地藏) "earth store." If he is indeed Ksitigarbha Bodhisattva, then everyone would know him for his great vow: "I vow to not attain

185

Buddhahood until the hells are empty." He is praised in the *Ten Wheels of Ksitigarbha Sutra* in the following verse:

> Firm in upholding the precepts like Mount Sumeru,
> Persevering and indestructible like a precious *vajra*,
> Patient and unmovable like the great earth.

The *Longevity of Ksitigarbha Sutra* says, "Ksitigarbha is just another name for the inherent mind of all living beings." Also in the *Longevity of Ksitigarbha Sutra*, the Buddha says the following:

> The perfect and bright mind is called "the [Dharma] wheel as one wishes." The mind free of worries is called "observing at ease." The mind that is infinite is called "great bodhisattva." The mind that is free of shape and form is called "great being."

Here the expression "observing at ease" is the same as *guan-zizai*, the name of Avalokitesvara. Sometimes Ksitigarbha praises Avalokitesvara and sometimes Avalokitesvara praises Ksitigarbha. We can view them as manifestations of the same Dharmakaya. With his praise, Dharanimdhara Bodhisattva is exhorting living beings to praise Avalokitesvara for his physical, verbal, and mental karma, his ability to liberate living beings from the seven calamities and three poisons, and his thirty-three manifestations.

The bodhisattvas who appear in the *Universal Gate Sutra* each represent a virtue. Aksayamati Bodhisattva, who posed the question which led to the extensive conversation about Avalokitesvara Bodhisattva's virtues, represents wisdom. Avalokitesvara Bodhisattva represents compassion, and Dharanimdhara Bodhisattva who praised the transmission of the teaching represents courage. It is through these three bodhisattvas that Avalokitesvara's vritues are made known.

The Aspirations of the Assembly

When the Buddha preached this chapter on the Universal Gate, the eighty-four thousand living beings assembled there all generated the aspiration to attain *anuttara-samyak-sambodhi*.

The Sanskrit term used to describe enlightenment in this instance is *anuttara-samyak-sambodhi*, "unsurpassed perfect enlightenment." This is one of the rare terms that remains untranslated in Chinese, but is instead transliterated as *anouduoluo sanmiao sanputi* (阿耨多羅三藐三菩提). After Sakyamuni Buddha finishes teaching, the text states that all eighty-four thousand members of the assembly generated the aspiration for enlightenment. Enlightenment is described as "perfect" and "unsurpassed," which are often used to describe the Buddha. Thus the aspiration for enlightenment expressed by the assembly can also be seen as the aspiration to attain Buddhahood.

Anuttara-samyak-sambodhi is considered the highest possible enlightenment, such that there is nothing greater. "Enlightenment" is a contrast to the unenlightened state of ordinary beings and the lesser attainments of non-Buddhist teachings. "Perfect" distinguishes supreme enlightenment from that of *sravakas* and *pratyekabuddhas*. The enlightenment of these two classes of practitioners does not include the perfect integration of ultimate truth and conventional truth. "Unsurpassed" distinguishes supreme enlightenment from the enlightenment of bodhisattvas, which has been realized in stages and will eventually be surpassed by *anuttara-samyak-sambodhi*. Though bodhisattvas are able to contemplate the equality of ultimate truth and conventional truth and are unaffected by the extremes of emptiness and existence, their realization is as of yet incomplete, like the moon just before it is full. Only the enlightenment of the Buddha can be considered unsurpassed, perfect enlightenment. This state of mind is often abbreviated simply as *bodhi*, which is also known as the mind of enlightenment, the mind of compassion, and the mind of the Buddha. Having heard the *Universal Gate Sutra*, the assembly of eighty-four thousand generated the aspiration to attain enlightenment which is perfect and unsurpassed. This shows the great wisdom, great compassion, and great courage of the assembly.

The eighty-four thousand living beings of the assembly represent the eighty-four thousand afflictions in our minds. So often we do not realize that we have Avalokitesvara Bodhisattva within our true mind. Without realizing our true mind, we allow these afflictions to sneak around and have their way. Now you have read about this wondrous and subtle practice whereby you can transform desire into compassion, anger into courage, and ignorance into wisdom. If you can do this, then the eighty-four thousand afflictions can be transformed into the Buddha's mind of perfect enlightenment.

In closing this commentary on the *Universal Gate Sutra*, it is hoped that readers not be confined by the definitions and explications of the sutra's words. To read sutras one must be mindful, and keep one's eyes alert. In closing, I would like to offer a dedication:

May this merit and virtue
Be universally offered to all,
So that we and all sentient beings
Will all attain Buddhahood together.

Homage to the great, compassionate Avalokitesvara Bodhisattva! Have compassion for us, and grant us protection!

Universal Gate Sutra

Chinese Text

觀世音菩薩普門品

Miao　Fa　Lian　Hua　Jing
妙　法　蓮　華　經

Guan　Shi　Yin　Pu　Sa　Pu　Men　Pin
觀　世　音　菩　薩　普　門　品

Er	Shi	Wu	Jin	Yi	Pu	Sa	Ji	Cong
爾	時	無	盡	意	菩	薩,	即	從

Zuo	Qi	Pian	Tan	You	Jian	He	Zhang	Xiang
座	起,	偏	袒	右	肩,	合	掌	向

Fo	Er	Zuo	Shi	Yan	Shi	Zun	Guan	Shi
佛,	而	作	是	言:	「世	尊!	觀	世

Yin	Pu	Sa	Yi	He	Yin	Yuan	Ming	Guan
音	菩	薩,	以	何	因	緣,	名	觀

Shi	Yin	Fo	Gao	Wu	Jin	Yi	Pu	Sa
世	音?」	佛	告	無	盡	意	菩	薩:

Shan	Nan	Zi	Ruo	You	Wu	Liang	Bai	Qian
「善	男	子!	若	有	無	量	百	千

Wan	Yi	Zhong	Sheng	Shou	Zhu	Ku	Nao	Wen
萬	億	眾	生,	受	諸	苦	惱,	聞

Shi	Guan	Shi	Yin	Pu	Sa	Yi	Xin	Cheng
是	觀	世	音	菩	薩,	一	心	稱

Ming 名，Guan 觀，Shi 世，Yin 音，Pu 菩，Sa 薩，Ji 即，Shi 時，Guan 觀

Qi 其，Yin 音，Sheng 聲，Jie 皆，De 得，Jie 解，Tuo 脫！Ruo 若，You 有

Chi 持，Shi 是，Guan 觀，Shi 世，Yin 音，Pu 菩，Sa 薩，Ming 名，Zhe 者，

She 設，Ru 入，Da 大，Huo 火，Huo 火，Bu 不，Neng 能，Shao 燒，You 由

Shi 是，Pu 菩，Sa 薩，Wei 威，Shen 神，Li 力，Gu 故。Ruo 若，Wei 為

Da 大，Shui 水，Suo 所，Piao 漂，Cheng 稱，Qi 其，Ming 名，Hao 號，Ji 即

De 得，Qian 淺，Chu 處。Ruo 若，You 有，Bai 百，Qian 千，Wan 萬，Yi 億

Zhong 眾，Sheng 生，Wei 為，Qiu 求，Jin 金、Yin 銀、Liu 瑠，Li 璃、Che 硨

Qu 磲、Ma 瑪，Nao 瑙、Shan 珊，Hu 瑚、Hu 琥，Po 珀、Zhen 真，Zhu 珠

Deng 等，Bao 寶，Ru 入，Yu 於，Da 大，Hai 海，Jia 假，Shi 使，Hei 黑

Feng 風,	Chui 吹	Qi 其	Chuan 船	Fang 舫,	Piao 漂	Duo 墮	Luo 羅	Cha 刹
Gui 鬼	Guo 國,	Qi 其	Zhong 中	Ruo 若	You 有	Nai 乃	Zhi 至	Yi 一
Ren 人,	Cheng 稱	Guan 觀	Shi 世	Yin 音	Pu 菩	Sa 薩	Ming 名	Zhe 者,
Shi 是	Zhu 諸	Ren 人	Deng 等,	Jie 皆	De 得	Jie 解	Tuo 脫	Luo 羅
Cha 刹	Zhi 之	Nan 難,	Yi 以	Shi 是	Yin 因	Yuan 緣,	Ming 名	Guan 觀
Shi 世	Yin 音。	Ruo 若	Fu 復	You 有	Ren 人,	Lin 臨	Dang 當	Bei 被
Hai 害,	Cheng 稱	Guan 觀	Shi 世	Yin 音	Pu 菩	Sa 薩	Ming 名	Zhe 者,
Bi 彼	Suo 所	Zhi 執	Dao 刀	Zhang 杖,	Xun 尋	Duan 段	Duan 段	Huai 壞,
Er 而	De 得	Jie 解	Tuo 脫。	Ruo 若	San 三	Qian 千	Da 大	Qian 千
Guo 國	Tu 土,	Man 滿	Zhong 中	Ye 夜	Cha 叉	Luo 羅	Cha 刹,	Yu 欲

Lai 來	Nao 惱	Ren 人，	Wen 聞	Qi 其	Cheng 稱	Guan 觀	Shi 世	Yin 音
Pu 菩	Sa 薩	Ming 名	Zhe 者，	Shi 是	Zhu 諸	E 惡	Gui 鬼	Shang 尚
Bu 不	Neng 能	Yi 以	E 惡	Yan 眼	Shi 視	Zhi 之，	Kuang 況	Fu 復
Jia 加	Hai 害？	She 設	Fu 復	You 有	Ren 人，	Ruo 若	You 有	Zui 罪，
Ruo 若	Wu 無	Zui 罪，	Chou 杻	Xie 械	Jia 枷	Suo 鎖，	Jian 檢	Xi 繫
Qi 其	Shen 身，	Cheng 稱	Guan 觀	Shi 世	Yin 音	Pu 菩	Sa 薩	Ming 名
Zhe 者，	Jie 皆	Xi 悉	Duan 斷	Huai 壞，	Ji 即	De 得	Jie 解	Tuo 脫。
Ruo 若	San 三	Qian 千	Da 大	Qian 千	Guo 國	Tu 土，	Man 滿	Zhong 中
Yuan 怨	Zei 賊，	You 有	Yi 一	Shang 商	Zhu 主，	Jiang 將	Zhu 諸	Shang 商
Ren 人，	Ji 齎	Chi 持	Zhong 重	Bao 寶，	Jing 經	Guo 過	Xian 險	Lu 路，

Qi	Zhong	Yi	Ren	Zuo	Shi	Chang	Yan	Zhu
其	中	一	人,	作	是	唱	言:	「諸

Shan	Nan	Zi	Wu	De	Kong	Bu	Ru	Deng
善	男	子,	勿	得	恐	怖,	汝	等

Ying	Dang	Yi	Xin	Cheng	Guan	Shi	Yin	Pu
應	當	一	心	稱	觀	世	音	菩

Sa	Ming	Hao	Shi	Pu	Sa	Neng	Yi	Wu
薩	名	號,	是	菩	薩	能	以	無

Wei	Shi	Yu	Zhong	Sheng	Ru	Deng	Ruo	Cheng
畏	施	於	眾	生;	汝	等	若	稱

Ming	Zhe	Yu	Ci	Yuan	Zei	Dang	De	Jie
名	者,	於	此	怨	賊,	當	得	解

Tuo	Zhong	Shang	Ren	Wen	Ju	Fa	Sheng	Yan
脫!」	眾	商	人	聞,	俱	發	聲	言:

Na	Mo	Guan	Shi	Yin	Pu	Sa	Cheng	Qi
「南	無	觀	世	音	菩	薩!」	稱	其

Ming	Gu	Ji	De	Jie	Tuo	Wu	Jin	Yi
名	故,	即	得	解	脫。	無	盡	意,

Guan	Shi	Yin	Pu	Sa	Mo	He	Sa	Wei
觀	世	音	菩	薩	摩	訶	薩,	威

Shen 神	Zhi 之	Li 力，	Wei 巍	Wei 巍	Ru 如	Shi 是。	Ruo 若	You 有
Zhong 眾	Sheng 生，	Duo 多	Yu 於	Yin 婬	Yu 欲，	Chang 常	Nian 念	Gong 恭
Jing 敬	Guan 觀	Shi 世	Yin 音	Pu 菩	Sa 薩，	Bian 便	De 得	Li 離
Yu 欲。	Ruo 若	Duo 多	Chen 瞋	Hui 恚，	Chang 常	Nian 念	Gong 恭	Jing 敬
Guan 觀	Shi 世	Yin 音	Pu 菩	Sa 薩，	Bian 便	De 得	Li 離	Chen 瞋。
Ruo 若	Duo 多	Yu 愚	Chi 癡，	Chang 常	Nian 念	Gong 恭	Jing 敬	Guan 觀
Shi 世	Yin 音	Pu 菩	Sa 薩，	Bian 便	De 得	Li 離	Chi 癡。	Wu 無
Jin 盡	Yi 意！	Guan 觀	Shi 世	Yin 音	Pu 菩	Sa 薩，	You 有	Ru 如
Shi 是	Deng 等	Da 大	Wei 威	Shen 神	Li 力，	Duo 多	Suo 所	Rao 饒
Yi 益，	Shi 是	Gu 故	Zhong 眾	Sheng 生，	Chang 常	Ying 應	Xin 心	Nian 念。

Ruo	You	Nü	Ren	She	Yu	Qiu	Nan	Li
若	有	女	人,	設	欲	求	男,	禮

Bai	Gong	Yang	Guan	Shi	Yin	Pu	Sa	Bian
拜	供	養	觀	世	音	菩	薩,	便

Sheng	Fu	De	Zhi	Hui	Zhi	Nan	She	Yu
生	福	德	智	慧	之	男;	設	欲

Qiu	Nü	Bian	Sheng	Duan	Zheng	You	Xiang	Zhi
求	女,	便	生	端	正	有	相	之

Nü	Su	Zhi	De	Ben	Zhong	Ren	Ai	Jing
女,	宿	植	德	本,	眾	人	愛	敬。

Wu	Jin	Yi	Guan	Shi	Yin	Pu	Sa	You
無	盡	意!	觀	世	音	菩	薩	有

Ru	Shi	Li	Ruo	You	Zhong	Sheng	Gong	Jing
如	是	力!	若	有	眾	生,	恭	敬

Li	Bai	Guan	Shi	Yin	Pu	Sa	Fu	Bu
禮	拜	觀	世	音	菩	薩,	福	不

Tang	Juan	Shi	Gu	Zhong	Sheng	Jie	Ying	Shou
唐	捐。	「是	故	眾	生,	皆	應	受

Chi	Guan	Shi	Yin	Pu	Sa	Ming	Hao	Wu
持	觀	世	音	菩	薩	名	號。	無

盡意！若有人受持六十

二億恆河沙菩薩名字，

復盡形供養飲食、衣服

臥具、醫藥，於汝意云何？

是善男子善女人功德

多不？」無盡意言：「甚多！世

尊！」佛言：「若復有人，受持

觀世音菩薩名號，乃至

一時禮拜供養，是二人

福，正等無異，於百千萬

Yi	Jie	Bu	Ke	Qiong	Jin	Wu	Jin	Yi
億	劫'	不	可	窮	盡。	無	盡	意!

Shou	Chi	Guan	Shi	Yin	Pu	Sa	Ming	Hao
受	持	觀	世	音	菩	薩	名	號,

De	Ru	Shi	Wu	Liang	Wu	Bian	Fu	De
得	如	是	無	量	無	邊	福	德

Zhi	Li	Wu	Jin	Yi	Pu	Sa	Bai	Fo
之	利。」	無	盡	意	菩	薩	白	佛

Yan	Shi	Zun	Guan	Shi	Yin	Pu	Sa	Yun
言:	「世	尊!	觀	世	音	菩	薩	云

He	You	Ci	Suo	Po	Shi	Jie	Yun	He
何	遊	此	娑	婆	世	界?	云	何

Er	Wei	Zhong	Sheng	Shuo	Fa	Fang	Bian	Zhi
而	為	眾	生	說	法?	方	便	之

Li	Qi	Shi	Yun	He	Fo	Gao	Wu	Jin
力,	其	事	云	何?」	佛	告	無	盡

Yi	Pu	Sa	Shan	Nan	Zi	Ruo	You	Guo
意	菩	薩:	「善	男	子!	若	有	國

Tu	Zhong	Sheng	Ying	Yi	Fo	Shen	De	Du
土	眾	生,	應	以	佛	身	得	度

Zhe 者,	Guan 觀	Shi 世	Yin 音	Pu 菩	Sa 薩	Ji 即	Xian 現	Fo 佛
Shen 身	Er 而	Wei 為	Shuo 說	Fa 法。」	Ying 應	Yi 以	Pi 辟	Zhi 支
Fo 佛	Shen 身	De 得	Du 度	Zhe 者,	Ji 即	Xian 現	Pi 辟	Zhi 支
Fo 佛	Shen 身	Er 而	Wei 為	Shuo 說	Fa 法;	Ying 應	Yi 以	Sheng 聲
Wen 聞	Shen 身	De 得	Du 度	Zhe 者,	Ji 即	Xian 現	Sheng 聲	Wen 聞
Shen 身	Er 而	Wei 為	Shuo 說	Fa 法。	Ying 應	Yi 以	Fan 梵	Wang 王
Shen 身	De 得	Du 度	Zhe 者,	Ji 即	Xian 現	Fan 梵	Wang 王	Shen 身
Er 而	Wei 為	Shuo 說	Fa 法;	Ying 應	Yi 以	Di 帝	Shi 釋	Shen 身
De 得	Du 度	Zhe 者,	Ji 即	Xian 現	Di 帝	Shi 釋	Shen 身	Er 而
Wei 為	Shuo 說	Fa 法;	Ying 應	Yi 以	Zi 自	Zai 在	Tian 天	Shen 身

De 得	Du 度	Zhe 者,	Ji 即	Xian 現	Zi 自	Zai 在	Tian 天	Shen 身
Er 而	Wei 為	Shuo 說	Fa 法。	Ying 應	Yi 以	Da 大	Zi 自	Zai 在
Tian 天	Shen 身	De 得	Du 度	Zhe 者,	Ji 即	Xian 現	Da 大	Zi 自
Zai 在	Tian 天	Shen 身	Er 而	Wei 為	Shuo 說	Fa 法;	Ying 應	Yi 以
Tian 天	Da 大	Jiang 將	Jun 軍	Shen 身	De 得	Du 度	Zhe 者,	Ji 即
Xian 現	Tian 天	Da 大	Jiang 將	Jun 軍	Shen 身	Er 而	Wei 為	Shuo 說
Fa 法;	Ying 應	Yi 以	Pi 毗	Sha 沙	Men 門	Shen 身	De 得	Du 度
Zhe 者,	Ji 即	Xian 現	Pi 毗	Sha 沙	Men 門	Shen 身	Er 而	Wei 為
Shuo 說	Fa 法。	Ying 應	Yi 以	Xiao 小	Wang 王	Shen 身	De 得	Du 度
Zhe 者,	Ji 即	Xian 現	Xiao 小	Wang 王	Shen 身	Er 而	Wei 為	Shuo 說

Fa	Ying	Yi	Zhang	Zhe	Shen	De	Du	Zhe
法;	應	以	長	者	身	得	度	者,

Ji	Xian	Zhang	Zhe	Shen	Er	Wei	Shuo	Fa
即	現	長	者	身	而	為	說	法;

Ying	Yi	Ju	Shi	Shen	De	Du	Zhe	Ji
應	以	居	士	身	得	度	者,	即

Xian	Ju	Shi	Shen	Er	Wei	Shuo	Fa	Ying
現	居	士	身	而	為	說	法;	應

Yi	Zai	Guan	Shen	De	Du	Zhe	Ji	Xian
以	宰	官	身	得	度	者,	即	現

Zai	Guan	Shen	Er	Wei	Shuo	Fa	Ying	Yi
宰	官	身	而	為	說	法;	應	以

Po	Luo	Men	Shen	De	Du	Zhe	Ji	Xian
婆	羅	門	身	得	度	者,	即	現

Po	Luo	Men	Shen	Er	Wei	Shuo	Fa	Ying
婆	羅	門	身	而	為	說	法。	應

Yi	Bi	Qiu	Bi	Qiu	Ni	You	Po	Se
以	比	丘、	比	丘	尼、	優	婆	塞、

You	Po	Yi	Shen	De	Du	Zhe	Ji	Xian
優	婆	夷	身	得	度	者,	即	現

Bi	Qiu	Bi	Qiu	Ni	You	Po	Se	You
比	丘、	比	丘	尼、	優	婆	塞、	優
Po	Yi	Shen	Er	Wei	Shuo	Fa	Ying	Yi
婆	夷	身	而	為	說	法。	應	以
Zhang	Zhe	Ju	Shi	Zai	Guan	Po	Luo	Men
長	者、	居	士、	宰	官	婆	羅	門、
Fu	Nü	Shen	De	Du	Zhe	Ji	Xian	Fu
婦	女	身	得	度	者,	即	現	婦
Nü	Shen	Er	Wei	Shuo	Fa	Ying	Yi	Tong
女	身	而	為	說	法。	應	以	童
Nan	Tong	Nü	Shen	De	Du	Zhe	Ji	Xian
男	童	女	身	得	度	者,	即	現
Tong	Nan	Tong	Nü	Shen	Er	Wei	Shuo	Fa
童	男	童	女	身	而	為	說	法。
Ying	Yi	Tian	Long	Ye	Cha	Qian	Ta	Po
應	以	天	龍、	夜	叉	乾	闥	婆、
O	Xiu	Luo	Jia	Lou	Luo	Jin	Na	Luo
阿	修	羅、	迦	樓	羅、	緊	那	羅、
Mo	Hou	Luo	Qie	Ren	Fei	Ren	Deng	Shen
摩	睺	羅	伽、	人	非	人	等	身

De 得　Du 度　Zhe 者,　Ji 即　Jie 皆　Xian 現　Zhi 之,　Er 而　Wei 為

Shuo 說　Fa 法。　Ying 應　Yi 以　Zhi 執　Jin 金　Gang 剛　Shen 神　De 得

Du 度　Zhe 者,　Ji 即　Xian 現　Zhi 執　Jin 金　Gang 剛　Shen 神　Er 而

Wei 為　Shuo 說　Fa 法。　Wu 無　Jin 盡　Yi 意!　Shi 是　Guan 觀　Shi 世

Yin 音　Pu 菩　Sa 薩,　Cheng 成　Jiu 就　Ru 如　Shi 是　Gong 功　De 德。

Yi 以　Zhong 種　Zhong 種　Xing 形,　You 遊　Zhu 諸　Guo 國　Tu 土,　Du 度

Tuo 脫　Zhong 眾　Sheng 生。　Shi 是　Gu 故　Ru 汝　Deng 等　Ying 應　Dang 當

Yi 一　Xin 心　Gong 供　Yang 養　Guan 觀　Shi 世　Yin 音　Pu 菩　Sa 薩,

Shi 是　Guan 觀　Shi 世　Yin 音　Pu 菩　Sa 薩　Mo 摩　He 訶　Sa 薩,

Yu 於　Bu 怖　Wei 畏　Ji 急　Nan 難　Zhi 之　Zhong 中,　Neng 能　Shi 施

Wu	Wei	Shi	Gu	Ci	Suo	Po	Shi	Jie
無	畏,	是	故	此	娑	婆	世	界,

Jie	Hao	Zhi	Wei	Shi	Wu	Wei	Zhe	Wu
皆	號	之	為	施	無	畏	者。	無

Jin	Yi	Pu	Sa	Bai	Fo	Yan	Shi	Zun
盡	意	菩	薩	白	佛	言:	「世	尊!

Wo	Jin	Dang	Gong	Yang	Guan	Shi	Yin	Pu
我	今	當	供	養	觀	世	音	菩

Sa	Ji	Jie	Jing	Zhong	Bao	Zhu	Ying	Luo
薩。」	即	解	頸	眾	寶	珠	瓔	珞

Jia	Zhi	Bai	Qian	Liang	Jin	Er	Yi	Yu
價	值	百	千	兩	金,	而	以	與

Zhi	Zuo	Shi	Yan	Ren	Zhe	Shou	Ci	Fa
之,	作	是	言:	「仁	者!	受	此	法

Shi	Zhen	Bao	Ying	Luo	Shi	Guan	Shi	Yin
施,	珍	寶	瓔	珞。」	時	觀	世	音

Pu	Sa	Bu	Ken	Shou	Zhi	Wu	Jin	Yi
菩	薩,	不	肯	受	之。	無	盡	意

Fu	Bai	Guan	Shi	Yin	Pu	Sa	Yan	Ren
復	白	觀	世	音	菩	薩	言:	「仁

Zhe 者!	Min 愍	Wo 我	Deng 等	Gu 故,	Shou 受	Ci 此	Ying 瓔	Luo 珞。」
Er 爾	Shi 時	Fo 佛	Gao 告	Guan 觀	Shi 世	Yin 音	Pu 菩	Sa 薩:
Dang 「當	Min 愍	Ci 此	Wu 無	Jin 盡	Yi 意	Pu 菩	Sa 薩,	Ji 及
Si 四	Zhong 眾	Tian 天	Long 龍	Ye 夜	Cha 叉	Qian 乾	Da 闥	Po 婆
O 阿	Xiu 修	Luo 羅、	Jia 迦	Lou 樓	Luo 羅、	Jin 緊	Na 那	Luo 羅
Mo 摩	Hou 睺	Luo 羅	Qie 伽、	Ren 人	Fei 非	Ren 人	Deng 等	Gu 故,
Shou 受	Ci 此	Ying 瓔	Luo 珞。」	Ji 即	Shi 時	Guan 觀	Shi 世	Yin 音
Pu 菩	Sa 薩,	Min 愍	Zhu 諸	Si 四	Zhong 眾,	Ji 及	Yu 與	Tian 天
Long 龍	Ren 人	Fei 非	Ren 人	Deng 等,	Shou 受	Qi 其	Ying 瓔	Luo 珞,
Fen 分	Zuo 作	Er 二	Fen 分:	Yi 一	Fen 分	Feng 奉	Shi 釋	Jia 迦

Mou	Ni	Fo	Yi	Fen	Feng	Duo	Bao	Fo
牟	尼	佛，	一	分	奉	多	寶	佛

Ta	Wu	Jin	Yi	Guan	Shi	Yin	Pu	Sa
塔。	「無	盡	意！	觀	世	音	菩	薩，

You	Ru	Shi	Zi	Zai	Shen	Li	You	Yu
有	如	是	自	在	神	力，	遊	於

Suo	Po	Shi	Jie	Er	Shi	Wu	Jin	Yi
娑	婆	世	界。」	爾	時，	無	盡	意

Pu	Sa	Yi	Ji	Wen	Yue
菩	薩	以	偈	問	曰 :

Shi	Zun	Miao	Xiang	Ju
「世	尊	妙	相	具 ，

Wo	Jin	Chong	Wen	Bi
我	今	重	問	彼 :

Fo	Zi	He	Yin	Yuan
佛	子	何	因	緣 ，

Ming	Wei	Guan	Shi	Yin
名	為	觀	世	音 ?」

Ju	Zu	Miao	Xiang	Zun
具	足	妙	相	尊 ，

Ji	Da	Wu	Jin	Yi	
偈	答	無	盡	意	。

Ru	Ting	Guan	Yin	Xing	
汝	聽	觀	音	行	，

Shan	Ying	Zhu	Fang	Suo	
善	應	諸	方	所	，

Hong	Shi	Shen	Ru	Hai	
弘	誓	深	如	海	，

Li	Jie	Bu	Si	Yi	
歷	劫	不	思	議	，

Shi	Duo	Qian	Yi	Fo	
侍	多	千	億	佛	，

Fa	Da	Qing	Jing	Yuan	
發	大	清	淨	願	。

Wo	Wei	Ru	Lue	Shuo	
我	為	汝	略	說	，

Wen	Ming	Ji	Jian	Shen	
聞	名	及	見	身	，

Xin	Nian	Bu	Kong	Guo	
心	念	不	空	過	，

Neng	Mie	Zhu	You	Ku	
能	滅	諸	有	苦	。

Jia	Shi	Xing	Hai	Yi	
假	使	興	害	意	，

Tui	Luo	Da	Huo	Keng	
推	落	大	火	坑	；

Nian	Bi	Guan	Yin	Li	
念	彼	觀	音	力	，

Huo	Keng	Bian	Cheng	Chi	
火	坑	變	成	池	。

Huo	Piao	Liu	Ju	Hai	
或	漂	流	巨	海	，

Long	Yu	Zhu	Gui	Nan	
龍	魚	諸	鬼	難	；

Nian	Bi	Guan	Yin	Li	
念	彼	觀	音	力	，

Bo	Lang	Bu	Neng	Mo	
波	浪	不	能	沒	。

Huo	Zai	Xu	Mi	Feng	
或	在	須	彌	峰	，

Wei	Ren	Suo	Tui	Duo	
為	人	所	推	墮	；

Nian	Bi	Guan	Yin	Li	
念	彼	觀	音	力	，

Ru	Ri	Xu	Kong	Zhu	
如	日	虛	空	住	。

Huo	Bei	E	Ren	Zhu	
或	被	惡	人	逐	，

Duo	Luo	Jin	Gang	Shan	
墮	落	金	剛	山	；

Nian	Bi	Guan	Yin	Li	
念	彼	觀	音	力	，

Bu	Neng	Sun	Yi	Mao	
不	能	損	一	毛	。

Huo	Zhi	Yuan	Zei	Rao	
或	值	怨	賊	繞	，

Ge	Zhi	Dao	Jia	Hai	
各	執	刀	加	害	；

Nian	Bi	Guan	Yin	Li	
念	彼	觀	音	力	，

Xian	Ji	Qi	Ci	Xin
咸	即	起	慈	心 。

Huo	Zao	Wang	Nan	Ku
或	遭	王	難	苦 ，

Lin	Xing	Yu	Shou	Zhong
臨	刑	欲	壽	終 ；

Nian	Bi	Guan	Yin	Li
念	彼	觀	音	力 ，

Dao	Xun	Duan	Duan	Huai
刀	尋	段	段	壞 。

Huo	Qiu	Jin	Jia	Suo
或	囚	禁	枷	鎖 ，

Shou	Zu	Bei	Chou	Xie
手	足	被	杻	械 ；

Nian	Bi	Guan	Yin	Li
念	彼	觀	音	力 ，

Shi	Ran	De	Jie	Tuo
釋	然	得	解	脫 。

Zhou	Zu	Zhu	Du	Yao
咒	詛	諸	毒	藥 ，

Suo	Yu	Hai	Shen	Zhe
所	欲	害	身	者 ；

Nian	Bi	Guan	Yin	Li
念	彼	觀	音	力 ，

Huan	Zhuo	Yu	Ben	Ren
還	著	於	本	人 。

Huo	Yu	E	Luo	Cha
或	遇	惡	羅	剎 ，

Du	Long	Zhu	Gui	Deng
毒	龍	諸	鬼	等 ；

Nian	Bi	Guan	Yin	Li
念	彼	觀	音	力 ，

Shi	Xi	Bu	Gan	Hai
時	悉	不	敢	害 。

Ruo	E	Shou	Wei	Rao
若	惡	獸	圍	繞 ，

Li	Ya	Zhua	Ke	Bu
利	牙	爪	可	怖 ；

Nian	Bi	Guan	Yin	Li
念	彼	觀	音	力 ，

Ji	Zou	Wu	Bian	Fang	
疾	走	無	邊	方	。

Yuan	She	Ji	Fu	Xie	
蚖	蛇	及	蝮	蝎	,

Qi	Du	Yan	Huo	Ran	
氣	毒	煙	火	然	;

Nian	Bi	Guan	Yin	Li	
念	彼	觀	音	力	,

Xun	Sheng	Zi	Hui	Qu	
尋	聲	自	迴	去	。

Yun	Lei	Gu	Che	Dian	
雲	雷	鼓	掣	電	,

Jiang	Bao	Shu	Da	Yu	
降	雹	澍	大	雨	;

Nian	Bi	Guan	Yin	Li	
念	彼	觀	音	力	,

Ying	Shi	De	Xiao	San	
應	時	得	消	散	。

Zhong	Sheng	Bei	Kun	E	
眾	生	被	困	厄	,

Wu	Liang	Ku	Bi	Shen
無	量	苦	逼	身 ;

Guan	Yin	Miao	Zhi	Li
觀	音	妙	智	力 ,

Neng	Jiu	Shi	Jian	Ku
能	救	世	間	苦 。

Ju	Zu	Shen	Tong	Li
具	足	神	通	力 ,

Guang	Xiu	Zhi	Fang	Bian
廣	修	智	方	便 ,

Shi	Fang	Zhu	Guo	Tu
十	方	諸	國	土 ,

Wu	Cha	Bu	Xian	Shen
無	刹	不	現	身 。

Zhong	Zhong	Zhu	E	Qu
種	種	諸	惡	趣 ,

Di	Yu	Gui	Chu	Sheng
地	獄	鬼	畜	生 ,

Sheng	Lao	Bing	Si	Ku
生	老	病	死	苦 ,

Yi	Jian	Xi	Ling	Mie	
以	漸	悉	令	滅	。

Zhen	Guan	Qing	Jing	Guan	
真	觀	清	淨	觀	,

Guang	Da	Zhi	Hui	Guan	
廣	大	智	慧	觀	,

Bei	Guan	Ji	Ci	Guan	
悲	觀	及	慈	觀	,

Chang	Yuan	Chang	Zhan	Yang	
常	願	常	瞻	仰	。

Wu	Gou	Qing	Jing	Quang	
無	垢	清	淨	光	,

Hui	Ri	Po	Zhu	An	
慧	日	破	諸	闇	,

Neng	Fu	Zai	Feng	Huo	
能	伏	災	風	火	,

Pu	Ming	Zhao	Shi	Jian	
普	明	照	世	間	。

Bei	Ti	Jie	Lei	Zhen	
悲	體	戒	雷	震	,

Ci	Yi	Miao	Da	Yun	
慈	意	妙	大	雲	，

Shu	Gan	Lu	Fa	Yu	
澍	甘	露	法	雨	，

Mie	Chu	Fan	Nao	Yan	
滅	除	煩	惱	燄	。

Zheng	Song	Jing	Guan	Chu	
諍	訟	經	官	處	，

Bu	Wei	Jun	Zhen	Zhong	
怖	畏	軍	陣	中	；

Nian	Bi	Guan	Yin	Li	
念	彼	觀	音	力	，

Zhong	Yuan	Xi	Tui	San	
眾	怨	悉	退	散	。

Miao	Yin	Guan	Shi	Yin	
妙	音	觀	世	音	，

Fan	Yin	Hai	Chao	Yin	
梵	音	海	潮	音	，

Sheng	Bi	Shi	Jian	Yin	
勝	彼	世	間	音	，

Shi	Gu	Xu	Chang	Nian				
是	故	須	常	念	。			

Nian	Nian	Wu	Sheng	Yi				
念	念	勿	生	疑	，			

Guan	Shi	Yin	Jing	Sheng				
觀	世	音	淨	聖	，			

Yu	Ku	Nao	Si	E				
於	苦	惱	死	厄	，			

Neng	Wei	Zuo	Yi	Hu				
能	為	作	依	怙	！			

Ju	Yi	Qie	Gong	De				
具	一	切	功	德	，			

Ci	Yan	Shi	Zhong	Sheng				
慈	眼	視	眾	生	，			

Fu	Ju	Hai	Wu	Liang				
福	聚	海	無	量	，			

Shi	Gu	Ying	Ding	Li				
是	故	應	頂	禮	。			

Er	Shi	Chi	Di	Pu	Sa	Ji	Cong	Zuo
爾	時	持	地	菩	薩，	即	從	座

起，前白佛言：「世尊！若有眾生，聞是觀世音菩薩品，自在之業，普門示現神通力者，當知是人，功德不少。」佛說是普門品時，眾中八萬四千眾生，皆發無等等阿耨多羅三藐三菩提心。

List of Texts

Venerable Master Hsing Yun extensively quotes the Buddhist sutras throughout his teachings, often sharing short passages from a staggering variety of works. If a reader is moved by a particular passage, the next step of visiting the literature itself can be a difficult one. An alphabetical list of sutras is provided below to assist in this process. The sutras are organized by their titles in English, except in such cases when the Sanskrit name of the text has become commonplace, as in the case of the *Dharmapada*. Each text is also listed with its common Chinese title, both in Chinese characters and pinyin pronunciation. Full Chines titles are listed in brackets.

Abhidharma Canon
    Apitan   阿毗曇

Amitabha Sutra
    Foshuo Amituo Jing   佛說阿彌陀經

Analysis and Appreciation of the Lotus Sutra
    Fahua Jing Xuanzan   法華經玄贊
    [妙法蓮華經玄贊]

Annotated Sayings of the Patriarchs
    Zuting Shiyuan   祖庭事苑

Annotations on the Meaning of the Lotus Sutra
    Fahua Yishu   法華義疏

Annotations to the Vimalakirti Sutra
    Weimo Jingzhu   維摩經註
    ［注維摩詰經］

Biography of Xuanzang
    Cien Zhuan   慈恩傳
    ［大唐大慈恩寺三藏法師傳］

Commentary on the Flower Adornment Sutra
    Huayan Shuchao   華嚴疏鈔

Commentary on the Verses from the Abhidharma
    Jushe Song Shu   俱舍頌疏
    ［俱舍論頌疏］

Complete Enlightenment Sutra
    Yuanjue Jing   圓覺經
    ［大方廣圓覺經］

Dharmapada
    Faju Jing   法句經

Diamond Sutra
    Jingang Jing   金剛經
    ［金剛般若波羅蜜經］

Eleven Faces Sutra
　　Shiyi Mian Jing   十一面經
　　［十一面觀世音神咒經］

Exegesis on the Words and Phrases in the Lotus Sutra
　　Fahua Wenju   法華文句
　　［妙法蓮華經文句］

Explanation of the Lotus Sutra
　　Miaofa Lianhua Jingjie   妙法蓮華經解
　　［妙法蓮華經要解］

Flower Adornment Sutra
　　Huayan Jing   華嚴經
　　［大方廣佛華嚴經］

Flower of Compassion Sutra
　　Beihua Jing   悲華經

Glossary of Translated Terms
　　Fanyi Mingyi Ji   翻譯名義集

Golden Light Sutra
　　Jin Guangming Jing   金光明經

Great Stopping and Seeing
　　Mohe Zhiguan   摩訶止觀

Huiyuan's Dictionary
Huiyuan Yinyi   慧苑音義
[新譯大方廣佛華嚴經音義]

Inquiry into the Profundity of the Flower Adornment Sutra
Huayan Tanxuan Ji   華嚴探玄記
[華嚴經探玄記]

Interpretation on Mind Contemplation
Guanxin Shi   觀心釋

Lion's Roar of Queen Srimala Sutra
Shengman Jing   勝鬘經

Lotus Sutra Commentary
Fahua Lun   法華論
[妙法蓮華經論優波提舍]

Lotus Sutra
Fahua Jing   法華經
[大乘妙法蓮華經]

Mantra Ritual
Zhenyan Yigui   真言儀軌

Miscellaneous Treasures Sutra
Za Baozang Jing   雜寶藏經

Necklace of Original Conduct Sutra
    Benye Yingluo Jing   本業瓔珞經
    ［菩薩瓔珞本業經］

Notes on the Meaning of Avalokitesvara
    Guanyin Yishu Ji   觀音義疏記

On Curbing Desire
    Eyu Wen   過欲文

One Hundred Parables Sutra
    Baiyu Jing   百喻經
    ［百句譬喻經］

Perfection of Great Wisdom Sutra
    Mohe Bore Jing   摩訶般若經
    ［摩訶般若波羅蜜多經］

Profound Meaning of the Lotus Sutra
    Fahua Xuanyi   法華玄義
    ［妙法蓮華經玄義］

Satya Nirgrantha Sutra
    Sazhe Niqianzi Jing   薩遮尼乾子經

Surangama Sutra
    Lengyan Jing   楞嚴經
    ［大佛頂首楞嚴經］

Sutra Asked by Visesacinta Brahma Deva
  Siyi Jing   思益經
  [思益梵天所問經]

Sutra in Forty-Two Sections
  Sishier Zhang Jing   四十二章經
  [佛說四十二章經]

Sutra of the Heavenly King Vaisravana
  Pishamen Tianwang Jing   毗沙門天王經

Sutra of the Pure Bodhisattva Avalokitesvara
  Qing Guanyin Jing   請觀音經
  [請觀世音菩薩消伏毒害陀羅尼咒經]

Sutra of the Teachings Bequeathed by the Buddha
  Fo Yijiao Jing   佛遺教經

Sutra on the Buddha of Infinite Life
  Wuliang Shou Jing   無量壽經
  [佛說無量壽經]

Sutra on the Contemplation of the Mind
  Xindi Guan Jing   心地觀經
  [大乘本生心地觀經]

Sutra on the Prophesized Enlightenment of
Avalokitesvara Bodhisattva
  Guanyin Shouji Jing   觀音授記經
  [觀世音菩薩授記經]

Ten Line Avalokitesvara Sutra
    Shiju Guanyin Jing   十句觀音經
    [延命十句觀音經]

Ten Part Vinaya
    Shi Song Lü   十誦律

Ten Wheels of Ksitigarbha Sutra
    Dizang Shilun Jing   地藏十輪經
    [大乘大集地藏十輪經]

The Longevity of Ksitigarbha Sutra
    Yanming Dizang Jing   延命地藏經
    [佛說延命地藏菩薩經]

Transcendent Sun and Moon Samadhi Sutra
    Chao Riyue Sanmei Jing   超日月三昧經
    [佛說超日明三昧經]

Treatise on Awakening of Faith in Mahayana
    Dacheng Qixin Lun   大乘起信論

Treatise on Consciousness Only
    Weishi Lun   唯識論
    [成唯識論]

Treatise on the Abhidharma
    Posuo Lun   婆娑論
    [阿毗達磨大毗婆娑論]

Treatise on the Mahayana Abhidharma
　　Ji Lun　　　　　　　　　　集論
　　[大乘阿毘達磨雜集論]

Treatise on the Perfection of Great Wisdom
　　Dazhi Du Lun　　　　　　　大智度論

Universal Gate Sutra
　　Pumen Pin　　　　　　　　普門品
　　[觀世音菩薩普門品]

Vajra Realm Mandala
　　Jingang Jie Mantuluo　　　金剛界曼荼羅

Vimalakirti Sutra
　　Weimo Jing　　　　　　　維摩經
　　[佛說維摩詰經]

Yuye Sutra
　　Yuye Jing　　　　　　　　玉耶經
　　[佛說玉耶女經]

Glossary

Abhidharma. Sanskrit for "higher doctrine." It is the philosophical treatment of the Buddha's teachings, and the third "basket" of the Buddhist Canon. The foundational Buddhist doctrine, known as the Tripitaka or "three baskets," are comprised of three types of teachings: the *sutras* or teachings and sayings of the Buddha, the *vinaya* or rules for monastics, and the *Abhidharma* or commentary.

Amitabha Buddha. The Buddha of boundless light and boundless life. Amitabha is one of the most popular Buddhas for devotion among Mahayana Buddhists. He presides over the Pure Land of Ultimate Bliss.

Buddha. Sanskrit for "awakened one." Though there are many Buddhas, the term typically refers to Sakyamuni Buddha, the historical Buddha and founder of Buddhism. Buddhahood is the attainment and expression that characterizes a Buddha and the ultimate goal of all sentient beings.

causes and conditions. *See under* **karma**.

Chan School of Buddhism. One of the schools of Chinese Buddhism, brought to China by Bodhidharma. It emphasizes the cultivation of intrinsic wisdom and teaches that enlightenment is clarifying the mind and seeing one's own true nature. A major tenet of the Chan School is that the Dharma is wordlessly transmitted from mind to mind.

dharma. Sanskrit for "truth." Refers to the Buddha's teachings, as well as the truth of the universe. When capitalized, it denotes both the ultimate truth and the teachings of the Buddha. When the term appears in lowercase, it refers to anything that can be thought of, experienced, or named; this usage is close in meaning to the concept of "phenomena."

emptiness. The concept that everything in the world arises due to dependent origination and has no permanent self or substance. All phenomena are said to be empty of an inherently independent self.

enlightenment. The state of awakening to the Ultimate Truth—freedom from all afflictions and sufferings.

Esoteric School of Buddhism. One of the three major traditions in Buddhism. Among the three major traditions—Theravada, Mahayana, and Esoteric—the Esoteric School was the one developed last in Indian Buddhism.

five precepts. The most fundamental set of Buddhist precepts, or rules of moral conduct, observed by lay and monastic Buddhists alike. They are to refrain from killing, to refrain from stealing, to refrain from sexual misconduct, to refrain from lying, and to refrain from consuming intoxicants. There are several sets of precepts, with the five precepts being the most basic and fundamental. There are also a set of eight precepts for practitioners on retreat, ten precepts for novice monastics, and 250 precepts and 348 for male and female monastics.

four great mountains of Chinese Buddhism. These are Wutai Shan (Five-Terraced Mountain), Emei Shan (High and Lofty Mountain), Jiuhua Shan (Nine Glories Mountain), and Putuo Shan (Mount Potalaka). These have been important sites for Buddhist pilgrimage. Each of the four sacred peaks is said to be home to a great bodhisattva, Manjusri, Samantabhadra, Ksitigarbha, and Avalokitesvara, respectively.

Four Noble Truths. A fundamental and essential teaching of Buddhism that describes the presence of suffering, the cause of suffering, the cessation of suffering, and the path leading to the cessation of suffering.

impermanence. One of the most basic truths taught by the Buddha. It is the concept that all conditioned phenomena will arise, abide, change, and disappear due to causes and conditions.

karma. All wholesome and unwholesome actions, speech, and thoughts and their effects. The term literally means "action," though it is much more commonly used to describe the entirety of the Buddhist view of cause and effect. The Buddha stated that the causes, conditions, and rebirth that we encounter in the future are effects of our previous thoughts, words, and deeds. The term "causes and conditions" is used to analyze causal relationships in a Buddhist context. In this form of analysis, a cause denotes the major factor which produces an effect. A condition is a factor whose presence allows for a cause to produce a given effect. In the cause and effect phenomena of the growth of a plant, the seed is the cause, the sprouting of the seed is the effect, and factors such as the soil, sunlight, and water are the necessary conditions.

Kumarajiva (344-413). Sino-Indian Buddhist monk and a prolific sutra translator. Many of his sutra translations are still commonly chanted in the Buddhist liturgy today.

Mahakasyapa. One of the ten great disciples of the Buddha. He is known as foremost in ascetic practices, and is considered the first patriarch of the Chan School of Buddhism.

Manjusri. The Bodhisattva of wisdom.

merit. Blessings that occur because of wholesome deeds.

Middle Way. The path between the extremes of hedonism and extreme asceticism taught by the Buddha.

Nagarjuna. Born in Southern India in the second or third century. He is the founder of the Madhyamika School and the author of many commentaries and treatises. His famous works include *Treatise on the Perfection of Great Wisdom*, *Treatise on the Middle Way*, the *Merits of Right Deeds Sutra*, and many more. Therefore, he was given the title "Master of a Thousand Commentaries." He is one of Buddhism's most influential philosophers.

nirvana. A state of perfect tranquility that is the ultimate goal of Buddhist practice. The original meaning of this word is "extinguished, calmed, quieted, tamed, or dead." In Buddhism, it refers to the absolute extinction of individual existence, or of all afflictions and desires; it is the state of liberation beyond birth and death.

non-duality. *See under* **emptiness**.

prajna. Sanskrit for "wisdom." Typically referring to a transcendent variety of wisdom that comes from seeing the true nature of reality. *Prajna* wisdom is considered the highest form of wisdom, the wisdom of insight into the true nature of all phenomena.

Saha World. Literally "land of endurance." It indicates the present world where we reside, which is full of suffering to be endured. The beings in this world endure suffering and afflictions due to their greed, anger, hatred, and ignorance. Also referred to as "*samsara*," or the cycle of birth and death. When sentient beings die, they are reborn into one of the six realms of existence: heaven, human, *asura*, animals, hungry ghost, and hell. The cycle continues as a result of one's karmic actions. Outside of the Saha World exist four additional realms: that of the *sravaka*, *pratekyabuddha*, bodhisattva, and Buddha. Taken together with the six realms previously mentioned they are called the ten realms.

Sakyamuni Buddha. Siddartha Gautama, the historical Buddha and founder of the religion known today as Buddhism. The name "Sakyamuni" means "sage of the Sakyans," which was the name of his clan. He was born the prince of Kapilavastu, son of King Suddhodana. At the age of twenty-nine, he left the royal palace and his family in search of the meaning of existence. At the age of thirty-five, he attained enlightenment under the *bodhi* tree. He then spent the next forty-five years expounding his teachings, which include the Four Noble Truths, the Noble Eightfold Path, the law of cause and effect, and dependent origination. At the age of eighty, he entered the state of *parinirvana.*

Sariputra. One of the ten great disciples of the Buddha. He is known as foremost in wisdom.

Tathagata. One of the ten epithets of a Buddha, literally translated as "Thus Come One," meaning the one who has attained full realization of "suchness," true essence, or actuality, i.e., the one dwelling in the absolute, beyond all transitory phenomena, so that he can freely come and go anywhere.

ten wholesome actions. The ten wholesome actions are no killing, no stealing, no sexual misconduct, no lying, no duplicity, no harsh words, no flattery, no greed, no anger, and no ignorance.

ten realms. *See under* **Saha World**.

Tiantai School of Buddhsim. One of the eight major schools of Chan Buddhism. Tiantai Buddhism was founded on the *Lotus Sutra* and emphasized balancing practice and study. One of the school's main principles is the triple truth derived from Nāgārjuna, which maintains that phenomena are empty of self-nature, phenomena exist provisionally from a worldly perspective, and that phenomena are both empty of existence and exist provisionally.

twelve links of dependent origination. Central Buddhist doctrine that all phenomena arise due to causes. There are twelve links that describe the series of causes by which old age and death arise in the world: Old age and death arise due to birth, birth arises due to becoming, becoming arises due to clinging, clinging arises due to craving, craving arises due to feeling, feeling arises due to contact, contact arises due to the six sense organs, the six sense organs arise due to name and form, name and form arise due to consciousness, consciousness arises due to mental formations, and mental formations arise due to ignorance.

Vasubandhu (320-380). Founded the Yogacara School of Buddhism, along with his brother, Asanga.

wheel of the Dharma. A symbol of the Buddha's teachings. The Dharma wheel rolls forth, crushing all delusions and afflictions. Its roundness is meant to symbolize perfection.

Xuanzang (602-664). Prolific Chinese Buddhist translator who traveled to India to recover Buddhist sutras. The events of his pilgrimage were fictionalized into the classic Chinese novel *Journey to the West.*

About the Author

Venerable Master Hsing Yun is a Chinese Buddhist monk, author, philanthropist, and founder of the Fo Guang Shan monastic order, which has branches throughout Asia, Europe, Africa, Australia, and the Americas. Ordained at the age of twelve in Jiangsu Province, China, Hsing Yun has spent over seventy years as a Buddhist monk building what he calls "Humanistic Buddhism"—Buddhism that meets the needs of people and is integrated into all aspects of daily life.

In 1949, Hsing Yun went to Taiwan and began to nurture the then burgeoning Buddhist culture on the island. Early on in his monastic career, he was involved in promoting Buddhism through the written word. He has served as an editor and contributor for many Buddhist magazines and periodicals, authoring the daily columns "Between Ignorance and Enlightenment," "Dharma Words," and "Hsing Yun's Chan Talk." In 1957, he started his own Buddhist magazine, *Awakening the World*, and in 2000, the first daily Buddhist newspaper, the *Merit Times*.

Hsing Yun has authored more than thirty books on how to bring happiness, peace, compassion and wisdom into daily life. These works include the *Song of Silence*, the *Biography of Sakyamuni Buddha*, and *National Master Yulin*. He also edited and published the *Fo Guang Encyclopedia*, the most authoritative Buddhist reference work in the Chinese language. His contributions have reached as far as sponsoring Buddhist music and art to creating Buddhist programming for television, radio, and the stage.

Hsing Yun resides at Fo Guang Monastery in southern Taiwan and continues to keep a very active schedule, attending numerous speaking engagements each year. In 2010 he delivered around 120 lectures and gave nearly 30 interviews for television and radio. He continues to write a daily column for the *Merit Times*, as well as to produce one-stroke calligraphy paintings. He is also the acting president of Buddha's Light International Association (BLIA), the worldwide lay Buddhist service organization.

About Buddha's Light Publishing

Buddha's Light Publishing offers quality translations of classical Buddhist texts as well as works by contemporary Buddhist teachers and scholars. We embrace Humanistic Buddhism, and promote Buddhist writing which is accessible, community-oriented, and relevant to daily life.

Founded in 1996 by Venerable Master Hsing Yun as the Fo Guang Shan International Translation Center, Buddha's Light Publishing seeks to continue Master Hsing Yun's goal of promoting the Buddha's teachings by fostering writing, art, and culture. Learn more by visiting www.blpusa.com.